KNIT ARTISTIC SHAWLS

15 SPECIAL COLOUR WORK SHAWL DESIGNS

EXCLUSIVE KNITTING INSTRUCTIONS FOR TRIANGULAR SHAWL CREATIONS

Bärbel Salet

Tuva Publishing

www.tuvapublishing.com

Address Merkez Mah. Cavusbasi Cad. No71

Cekmekoy - Istanbul 34782 / Turkey

Tel +9 0216 642 62 62

Knit Artistic Shawls

First Print 2023 / June

All Global Copyrights Belong To
Tuva Tekstil ve Yayıncılık Ltd.

Content Knitting

Editor in Chief Ayhan DEMİRPEHLİVAN

Project Editor Kader DEMİRPEHLİVAN

Designer Bärbel SALET

Technical Editor Leyla ARAS

Graphic Designers Ömer ALP, Abdullah BAYRAKÇI,
Tarık TOKGÖZ, Yunus GÜLDOĞAN

Translater: Elisabeth M. STEINACHER

ISBN 978-605-7834-71-3

Copyright © 2022 Bärbel Salet and Stiebner Verlag GmbH
Text: Bärbel Salet
Photos of projects and models: Monika Tambour
Photos of instructions: Bernd Salet
Original title: Kunstvolle Tücher
First published by Stiebner Verlag GmbH, Germany

 TuvaYayincilik    TuvaPublishing

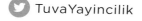 TuvaYayincilik    TuvaPublishing

CONTENTS

PROJECTS

PREFACE

A long-cherished dream came true when Melanie Stiebner proposed a book project to me: the idea to share my passion for colourwork knitting with other knitters and to present it to a larger circle of people makes me very happy.

Since many years ago I have been creating knitwear designs and I draw a lot of joy from combining gradient colours and designing matching patterns. Rather quickly I developed the idea to present large triangular shawls in this book, as these are my greatest passion.

This book features patterns and designs which have been published already - these were reinterpreted by my test knitters in new colour variations. Of course, I specially developed new models for this book, whereby the two following principles were of great importance to me:

I have designed shawls, which are suitable for beginners but I also created new patterns, which do offer a challenge even to experienced knitters. With this book I endeavour to address all levels and to arouse all knitters' curiosity. It is not really difficult - so have the heart to start!

Another aspect is that wearing a colourful shawl is definitely not limited to one single age group. No matter whether young or old - there are no limits. A self-confident attitude is of great importance: "I do like these colours and they make me feel good!" The key is your personal feeling!

During my workshops I have often been asked how I come up with ideas for the colour gradients. This is a topic, which I would like to also explain in detail in this book. We are surrounded by such a vast variety of colours, that ideas for themed colour arrangements do appear quite easily.

It is also important to me that colourwork knitting does not necessarily mean to be loud and multicoloured. I will also present colour variations which belong to the rather discreet and powder colour palettes. No matter whether autumnal, true summer, dark winter or bright spring - I'd like to show as many different colour gradient schemes as possible. All shawl patterns were knit in two different colour schemes in order to point out and at the same time stimulate creative flexibility. Thus, each and every shawl created will become one of a kind. Freely adapted from and true to the motto: Life is colourful!

I hope I could arise your curiosity so that you will enjoy both reading and knitting...

Bärbel Salet

THANK YOU

My dream of having my own knitting book published has finally come true and I would like to express my heartfelt thanks to all of those involved for their truly unwavering support. This project could not have come into being without the participation of many dear people.

A big thank you goes to Melanie Stiebner, who offered me this opportunity and devoted her time to me. Thanks to Steffi Klapetek for the wonderfully warm cooperation during the editing process, Thorsten Duit for his recommendation, Monika Tambour for the very sensitive and creative photo work and thanks also to my aunt Anna-Maria and my niece Charlotte for presenting the shawls.

Thanks to my test knitters it was possible that the large number of shawls presented in this book could be handknit in no time. The fruitful and creative exchange made me feel very warm at heart and grateful at the same time. Thank you for your accuracy and assistance in troubleshooting. Without you, quite a number of errors would still be present – as "one can't see the wood for trees" ... Andrea, Ulrike, Sonja, Bärbel, Sabine and Karin – you are just brilliant!

I would also like to thank my "gal pals" – that is Bea, Heike, Marlies, Sabine and Saskia – from the bottom of my heart for supporting me by test knitting the shawls. Thanks a million for your relentless motivation and unwavering friendship.

Thank you, dear Petra, for helping me along and thank you, dear Christine, for your good advice always and in more than one respect.

I would like to thank my sisters Uschi and Irene: you are always by my side!

And last but not least I would like to thank my husband Bernd and our son Marc Luca: you are my harshest critics. I love you.

BÄRBEL SALET

PROJECT GALLERY

Fire Lilies
P. 38

Gingko
P. 46

Fan Flowers
P. 54

Arabesque
P. 62

Tracery
P. 70

Vineyard
P. 78

Easygoing
P. 86

Gondwana
P. 94

Play of the Seasons
P. 102

Rise Like a Phoenix
P. 110

Rosana
P. 118

Spirelli
P. 126

Botanico
P. 134

Biggi
P. 144

Dahlias
P. 152

COLOURS

My great passion is creating colour gradients. Over the past years I have built up a collection of more than 360 different shades of yarn in my studio. This huge variety of colours allows me to create colour gradients without harsh transitions. Compiling such gradients and developing new patterns fills me with great joy. The close contact with my customers is very important to me and I would like to help them create their individual colour combinations. Every person is different and so are her or his personal colours.

Life is colourful!!

In the past I have held over fifty workshops concerning colourwork knitting. Out of experience, the participants can be divided in two groups. One group wants to learn more about the technical aspects of knitting my shawls and the other group wants to learn how to compile gradients. More often than not, this is also accompanied by the wish to break out of the usual colour comfort zone.

At the beginning of my workshops, I usually recommend the exercise to intuitively approach the colour range that corresponds to one's personal preferences. For this I normally prepare a large table for displaying yarn balls in different colours. During the exercise, it very often becomes clear that there is a tendency towards one's favourite colours, as these colours are contained within us, we feel comfortable with them and want to use them in our knitting. Nevertheless, the desire for colour changes does remain.

More often than not, change happens in small steps. One workshop participant intuitively picked her favourite blue shades, but actually wanted to try out the colour combination of green, red, orange and pink. I recommended that the knit a shawl in subtle shades of blue and use the new colours of her choice as eyecatchers in the border. The result was an absolutely gorgeous one-of-a-kind piece.

Those who do not have the possibility to choose from numerous coloured yarn balls, can always develop an eye for colour combinations by simply perceiving one's environment in a more conscious way. Colour combinations of all kinds can not only be found in nature, but also in photographs or in paintings by famous artists.

One day, for example, I discovered a postcard with a view of Paris in November rain. The eyecatcher was a lady carrying a yellow umbrella. Such eyecatchers are very important to me. We all know colours that are rather discreet, if not almost boring - but these are important "teammates", who will let stronger colours stand out and shine.

The following examples may provide you with some ideas and stimuli.

Where does inspiration come from?

I often find inspiration in nature, but also during numerous travels I have been able to collect quite a number of ideas for colour combinations and patterns.

While browsing the web, I discovered photos taken during a wedding. The bridesmaids were wearing purple dresses and their flower bouquets were tied entirely in purple and orange. This beautiful colour combination finally resulted in my Fan Flowers shawl.

During a trip through the south of England I discovered a turquoise door in a brick wall - and the idea for my Easygoing shawl was born.

© AdobeStock

© Bernd Salet

© Melanie Steiner

I also love the inspiration for the Gondwana shawl, which contains the colours nature, beige, green and turquoise. I discovered a photo of Uncle Titus - a chameleon! - in my friend Melanie's online status. These colours are still fascinating me!

My design and inspiration for the Biggi shawl also features quite a very special story. Biggi lives in New Zealand. We had already been in contact for a long time, when I discovered her post on Instagram. She was on a cycling tour, reported a bicycle breakdown - and was wearing the most colourful cycling jersey (©Cycology). The colours fascinated me to such an extent, that I simply had to use them for one of my shawls.

© Bernd Salet

© Biggi Spahn

9

TECHNIQUES NEEDED FOR THE SHAWLS

In this chapter I will describe all the individual steps needed for successfully knitting a large triangular shawl - they form the basis for all shawls contained in this book.

First and foremost, I would like to explain the knitting techniques on which all my experience is based. These are recommendations only - certainly not a must!

Maybe you have already knitted one or more large triangular shawls and are happy with your personal knitting technique. No problem at all - stick to your method! This is the only way to gain confidence and ensure you will have fun and can relax at the same time while knitting your shawl.

For all other knitters, who may have never before knitted a large triangular shawl, I will explain in this technical part in detail and based on the Easygoing shawl, how easy it is to knit a large triangular shaw.

Maybe you will have to familiarize yourself with some of my expressions: out of experience I know that my method of "purl bump increases" is not known at all, resulting in a number of questions during my workshops. Let me assure you that with all the photos and detailed descriptions of my preferred knitting technique, you will find your way around and manage!

All of my large triangular shawls are at the beginning knitted back and forth in rows. Once you have reached a total of 43 stitches and 23 rows, then the steek stitches are cast on and the rows are closed to a round. Now you may then either change to DPNs or with circular needles with long cables for making use of the Magic Loop method. You will find numerous online tutorials concerning this method (e.g., on YouTube).

General technique

There are two colour ranges in colourwork knitting: the background colour gradient (BC) and the pattern colour gradient (PC). In the diagrams and charts the pattern is represented by an "x". The background colours have not been allocated any symbol.

TIP: If you find the charts contained in this book to be too small to work with, you might want to enlarge them by using the photocopier's "Enlarge" button (e.g., from A4 to A3) to prepare a larger copy. This will make the chart easier to read.

Holding the yarn

There are a number of methods of holding the yarns. Here we must not distinguish between "right" and "wrong" but rather label these methods as being "different". Most knitters will quickly discover the way which suits them best. At the beginning, it is best to simply try out, which method is the best for you personally.

The two most common methods are to either hold both yarns in the left hand or hold one yarn in the left (background colour) and the other yarn in the right (pattern colour) hand (see figures 01 and 02). ▼

Figure 01: Both yarns in the left hand

Figure 02: One yarn in each hand

Catching/Trapping floats

Depending on the pattern, long floats may exist on the wrong side of your knitted shawl. It is therefore strongly recommended, to catch or trap these floats behind the work, especially if they are longer than four stitches. The following photos illustrate this method in more detail:

The pattern colour yarn is placed over the background colour yarn so that both yarns form a cross.
(see figure 03) ▼

Figure 03: Place/cross PC yarn over BC yarn

After having knit two or three stitches with BC according to the pattern, bring the PC yarn back to its original position
(see figure 04) ➤

Swatching

With many knitters, swatching is not really popular. During my workshops I am regularly being asked whether swatching is really necessary.

Generally speaking, it is advisable to knit swatches before beginning to knit a piece. Personally, I do knit most of my jumpers or cardigans with 3.0 mm needles, as this renders the knitted structure a little bit firmer. My shawls, however, I usually knit with 3.25 mm needles so that the knitted fabric will fall loosely from the shoulders as it is not desirable for a shawl to "behave" like a wooden board.

When knitting a large triangular shawl, swatching comes in quite useful in order to approximately achieve the final dimensions of such shawl. In contrast to a well-made jumper, it is not crucial whether a shawl in the end features a top wingspan of 220 cm or 225 cm.

Therefore, the dimensions of a shawl can vary slightly depending on the individual gauge. My swatching gauge with 3.25 mm needles (2 colour stranded knitting; stockinette stitch) usually results in 27 stitches x 32 rows for a 10 cm x 10 cm swatch.

Figure 04: Cross back PC yarn to its
original position

Arrangement of colours

My knitting kits contain colour cards, which clearly show the colour gradients - it is therefore easy to see which order should be followed. If you wish to knit your shawl with yarn readily available in your personal stash, then the compilation of a colour chart is recommended. Such a colour chart comes in handy especially if you wish to gain a first insight into how the colour gradients will look like. Should you wish to prepare your own "magic ball", you can easily jot down notes right on the colour card or take note of the number of rows to knit per colour.

Arranging colours by rows

Let's assume your shawl features a total of 300 rows/ round and you'll use 15 different colours for the whole shawl, then you might arrive at the following calculation: 300 rows divided by 15 = 20 rows

Thus, each colour will be assigned 20 rows for the entire shawl, provided that each colour will only be used once. If you plan to knit the gradient twice, then each colour is assigned 2 x 10 rows.

In the case of 4 colour repeats, each colour will be assigned 5 rows only.

Naturally, accents can also be added according to the principle of "artistic license" assigning more or less rows to each colour.

"Magic balls"

In order not to be forced to constantly check the colour chart for which colour has to be used next and to avoid the constant counting of rows, I'd recommend that you prepare "magic balls".

How to prepare a "magic ball"?

Each shawl starts by casting on three stitches and by continuously increasing in each and every row, the shawls feature much more than 500 stitches per row at the upper end. Therefore, the length of yarn per colour needed at the beginning of the shawl is much less than at the wide upper end.

In order to assign the correct amount of yarn, the yarn is measured in wingspans. One wingspan reaches from one hand to the other with arms stretched out. This is quite similar to the wingspan of a bird.

For the Easygoing shawl the colour gradient of the background colours (terracotta-rust-orange) starts with the colour "Jam. Ginger" and ends with "R. Henna". I jotted down the relevant wingspans on the colour card (see Figure 05) and assigned one wingspan to "Jam. Ginger". The number of wingspans is increased after every three colours, so that "R. Henna" is assigned 4 wingspans.

In order to start the shawl with "Jam. Ginger", this yarn colour must appear on the outside of the "magic ball" which in turn means, that I start winding the "magic ball" in reverse order:
First of all, 4 wingspans "R. Henna" are being measured and wound into a mini ball, then 4 wingspans of "Jam. Paprika" are measured and added to the mini ball (please ensure that the yarn is loosely wound), followed by 4 wingspans of "Har. Topaz" etc. until the ball can be finished with 1 wingspan of "Jam. Ginger".
Joining the single threads by knotting or felting them together can be done during the knitting process.

In order to create the second "magic ball", all wingspans have to be increased accordingly as the number of stitches per colour will increase by regularly casting on new stitches. That means if the last colour of the 1st "magic ball" sported 4 wingspans, you will have to continue with 5 wingspans of the following colour.

Figure 05: Colour chart and "magic ball"

TIP: First wrap the colour gradient once and jot down the wingspans on your colour chart so that it becomes very clear, which wingspans are required for the 2nd colour cycle. I personally would then start right knitting right away with the first "magic ball" - if necessary or desired, you might want to adjust or vary the wingspans a little bit. Artistic license!

For the "magic balls" to be used as the yarn for the pattern colour, the procedure is basically the same. However, for the Easygoing shawl please note there exists a special feature.

The first colour cycle starts with the colour "K. Larkspur" and ends with "LT#435 Eiswasser" (see figure 06).

However, the 2nd cycle starts again with the colour "LT#435 Eiswasser" and ends with "K. Larkspur". This means that the colour gradient is knitted back and forth, so that the colour "LT#435 Eiswasser" creates quite powerful highlights - these I also like to call eyecatchers.

When winding the "magic ball" for the first colour cycle, I start with the colour "LT#435 Eiswasser" (3 wingspans) and finish with the colour "K. Larkspur" (1 wingspan.)

For the second colour cycle I start winding the ball with the colour "K. Larkspur" (6 wingspans) and end with the colour "LT#435 Eiswasser" (4 wingspans).

Of course, the above method to prepare a "magic ball" is definitely an optional one. It is also possible to wind balls with any old length of yarn just the way you like it. The "counted" wingspan method on the other hand results in a certain continuous sequence, which in turn will provide you with rather harmonic colour transitions.

I truly do like to knit with "magic balls" as it is always and simply fascinating to see how the colour gradient develops during the knitting process. Another advantage is that you only need to carry 2 balls of yarn if you are for example a travelling knitter - namely one ball for the background colour scheme and one ball for the pattern colour scheme.

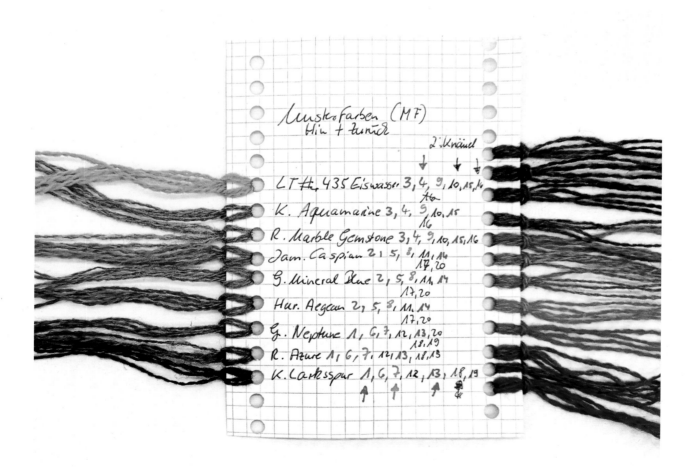

Figure 06: Colour chart for the pattern colour

Abbreviations

Code	Description
[|]	cast-on 1 stitch
[+]	increase by knitting into the purl bump
[A]	chain cast-on 1 stitch
[o]	knit stitch (chain casted-on in previous row)
BC	background colour(s)
GG	gauge
inc	increase
K / k	knit
k2tog	knit 2 together (right leaning decrease)
kfb	knit front and back (increase that uses 1 stitch to make 2 sts) knit into a stitch without taking it off the left-hand needle (you now have a loop on both the right and left needle), knit into the same stitch again through the back loop and take it off the left-hand needle
LFT / lft	left
M1L	make one left (left-leaning increase) pick up the bar between the stitch you knit and the one you are about to knit, bringing the needle from front to back; insert the tip of the right needle knit-wise into the back leg of the strand and knit
M1R	make one right (right-leaning increase) use the left needle to pick up the strand between the last stitch you knit and the one you're about to knit, bringing the needle from back to front, leave the strand on the left needle; insert the tip of the right needle knit-wise into the front leg of the strand and knit as usual
PC	pattern colour(s)
R / r	row(s)
Rd / rd	round(s)
RS / (RS)	right side row
RT / rt	right
SM	stitch marker
span	wingspan (wingspans are measured from hand to hand with arms stretched out completely, similar to the wingspan of a bird)
SS	selvedge stitch
ssk	slip, slip, knit (left-leaning decrease) slip 2 sts knitwise, then slide the left-hand needle into the front parts of both stitches and knit them together through the back loops
st(s)	stitch(es)
steek st(s)	steek stitch(es)
WS / (WS)	wrong side row

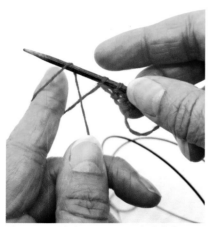

Figure 07: Chain cast-on 1 stitch [A]

Figure 08: 5 sts on the needle after row 4

Figure 09: Inc 1st by knitting into the purl bump

Starting your shawl

BC = magic ball "red-terracotta-orange"
PC = magic ball "blue, turquois, teal, mint"

R 1 (cast-on row): cast-on 3 sts with 3.25 mm or adjust needle size to obtain gauge (I prefer the long-tail cast-on).

R 2 (WS): purl 3 sts = 3 sts
Chain cast-on 1 st [A] (see figure 07) ▲ and turn work.

R 3 (RS): k first st (chain cast-on in previous row) [o] and k 3 sts = 4 sts
Chain cast-on 1 st [A] and turn work.

R 4 (WS): k first st [o] and p 4 sts = 5 sts (see figure 08) ▲,
Chain cast-on 1 st [A] and turn work.

Starting with R 5 (RS) it is of utmost importance that 1 st each is increased at the beginning (always k the cast-on stitch) and at the end (increase by knitting into the "purl bump") of each row - else the desired top width of the shawl cannot be achieved.

R 5 (RS) also marks the start of the pattern (PC) - please see Chart 1.

Increase 1 st by knitting into the "purl bump" (see figure 09): ▲
» With your left-hand needle, go into the "purl bump" of the chain cast-on stich of the previous row.
» Pick up a yarn with the left-hand needle.
» Knit the stitch with your right-hand needle.

Row 5 (RS)

» K first st [o]
» K 2 sts in BC
» K 1 st [x] in PC
» K 2 sts in BC
» Inc 1 st [+] by knitting into the "purl bump" (see figure 09) = 7 sts
» Chain cast-on 1 st [A] and turn work.

Why use the "purl bump" increase method?
The border will turn out to be much "neater" as the steps generated by simply increasing 2 stitches tend to be rather unattractive.

TIP: Alternatively, you may increase 1 st by M1R between the first and second stitch and increase 1 st by M1L between the penultimate and last stitch of each row.

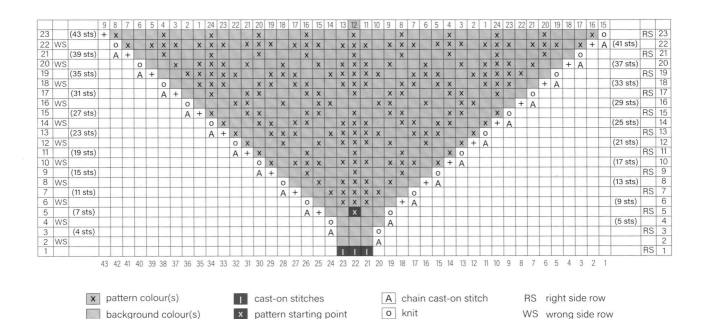

	x	pattern colour(s)		I	cast-on stitches		A	chain cast-on stitch	RS	right side row
		background colour(s)		x	pattern starting point		o	knit	WS	wrong side row
							+	purl bump increase		

Figure 10 / Chart 1: Arrangement of background colours (BC) and pattern colours (PC)

R 6 (WS)
» K first st [o]
» P 2 sts in BC
» P 3 sts in PC
» P 2 sts in BC
» Inc 1 st [+]
» Chain cast-on 1 st [A] and turn work.

K R 7 (RS) up to and including R 14 (WS) according to Chart 1 ∧

The pattern repeat for the Easygoing Shawl consists of 24 sts. These are aligned centrally. Once you have reached one full pattern repeat, I recommend to place one SM at the beginning and at the end for easier orientation.

Starting with R 15 (27 sts), the pattern is continuously extended both to the right and left side of the central pattern repeat.

Work R 16 (RS) up to and including R 23 (WS/43 sts) forth (RS) and back (WS) according to Chart 1.

Once R 23 (RS) is done, the beginning of the shawl is complete. (see figure 11) ▼

Figure 11: 43 sts at the end of R 23 (RS)

Integration of steek stitches

(see figure 12) ➤

» You have already completed the "purl bump" increase at the end of R 23 (RS) = 43 sts
» Place SM
» Chain cast-on 15 sts for the steek, alternating between BC and PC (always start with BC, so that the 1st and 15th steek sts are knit in BC). These stitches will serve as the basis for the border sts to be picked up.
» Join the row to a round.

My preferred method is the magic loop method. Of course, you can also use DPNs and change to circular needles with a 40 cm cable at a later stage. From now onwards, you will only use knit stitches.

Please change to the larger pattern now (Chart 2 ⌄ and continue with R 24.

Figure 12: 43 sts plus 15 steek stitches

	24	23	22	21	20	19	18	17	16	15	14	13	12	11	10	9	8	7	6	5	4	3	2	1	
24	X	X		X			X			X		X	X	X		X			X			X		X	24
23	X			X				X				X				X				X					23
22	X	X		X	X	X		X	X	X		X	X	X		X	X	X		X	X	X		X	22
21	X			X				X				X				X				X					21
20	X	X		X			X			X		X	X	X		X			X			X		X	20
19	X	X	X			X	X	X			X	X	X	X	X			X	X	X			X	X	19
18	X	X			X	X		X	X			X	X	X			X	X		X	X			X	18
17	X			X	X				X	X			X			X	X				X	X			17
16			X	X			X			X	X				X	X			X			X	X		16
15	X			X	X				X	X			X			X	X				X	X			15
14	X	X			X	X		X	X			X	X	X			X	X		X	X			X	14
13	X	X	X			X	X	X			X	X	X	X	X			X	X	X			X	X	13
12	X	X		X			X			X		X	X	X		X			X			X		X	12
11	X			X				X				X				X				X					11
10	X	X		X	X	X		X	X	X		X	X	X		X	X	X		X	X	X		X	10
9	X			X				X				X				X				X					9
8	X	X		X			X			X		X	X	X		X			X			X		X	8
7	X	X	X			X	X	X			X	X	X	X	X			X	X	X			X	X	7
6	X	X			X	X		X	X			X	X	X			X	X		X	X			X	6
5	X			X	X				X	X			x			X	X				X	X			5
4			X	X			X			X	X				X	X			X			X	X		4
3	X			X	X				X	X			X			X	X				X	X			3
2	X	X		X	X		X	X			X	X	X			X	X		X	X				X	2
1	X	X	X			X	X	X			X	X	X	X	X			X	X	X			X	X	1
	24	23	22	21	20	19	18	17	16	15	14	13	12	11	10	9	8	7	6	5	4	3	2	1	

Figure 13 / Chart 2: Pattern repeat

First round with steek stitches

You have joined the 43 regular and the 15 steek sts to a round. The yarns are now at the beginning of the round.

Start knitting with the following partition (Chart 2):

» Rd 24: knit the last 10 sts of the pattern repeat (from st 15 to st 24 inclusive).
» Move SM to the right needle.
» Knit the 24 sts of the starting centre repeat.
» Move SM.
» Knit the first 9 sts of the pattern repeat.
» You are now at the end of the row.

» Move SM to the right needle.
» Knit 14 steek sts according to the established colour scheme (as previously cast-on) so that a pattern of longitudinal lines is created. Such a steek will be more elastic and can be blocked easier. Therefore, please do not knit any checkerboard pattern.
» Place SM.
» Knit the 15ᵗʰ steek st.

This first round does not feature any increase at all.

From Rd 25 onwards and all following rounds
(See figure 14) ▼

The pattern repeat is 24 sts wide and 24 rounds high.

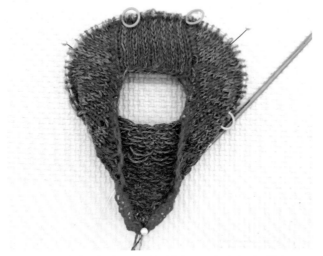

Figure 14: Knitting in the round with integrated steek stitches

I have often been asked how the following pattern repeats are to be generated and how these should be knitted. Many knitters are especially bothered by the pattern repeats on the left side of the steek as they rarely start with stitch 1 but the starting stitch must be determined by counting from right to left.

EXAMPLE: As shown in figure 15, the light-blue pattern repeat over 24 sts has been completed already. The stitches (yellow boxes; top right) are counted from right to left, starting from the position of the stitch marker.
So, stitches are counted backwards from st 24 over st 23 etc., until the starting stitch for the new round is reached. According to the chart, that would be st 19.

The first repeats of the pattern will thus develop as follows: (see figure 15) ▼

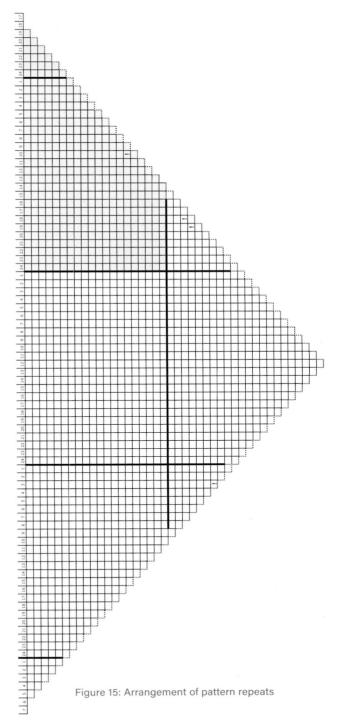

Figure 15: Arrangement of pattern repeats

Once a pattern repeat has been completed, it is recommended to mark it with a SM.
Once the 24th round has been completed, then the pattern is to be continued with 1st round.

» K all sts as per Chart 2/R 1.
» At the end of the rd (see figure 16) ➤ inc 1 st by kfb from the last stitch.
» Move SM to the right needle.
» K 14 steek sts.
» Move SM to the right needle.
» Inc 1 st by kfb from the 15th steek stitch (see figure 17) ➤

Extend the pattern to the right and left as you continuously add increases in each row. For better orientation, completed pattern repeats should be identified by the placement of SMs. In the end the shawl will be 578 sts wide and 292 rounds high.

The breakdown is as follows:
The pattern will be repeated altogether 23 times (23 x 24 sts = 552 sts).
The last 13 sts of the repeat are knitted at the right-hand side upper tip and the first 13 sts of the repeat are knitted on the left-hand side upper tip = 578 sts.

12 x 24 rows of the complete pattern repeat = 288 rds
1 x 4 rows of the pattern repeat (1st until 4th rd inclusive) = 4 rds
Total 292 rds

Securing the steek

Bind off steek sts 2 until 14 inclusive (see figure 18). ➤

The 1st and 15th steek stitches remain on the needles, as these are needed for knitting the border.
Moisten and block the steek.

TIP: An ironing board comes in handy for blocking the steek. Because of the uncut steek, the shawl now still resembles a loop - so it can easily be pulled over an ironing board.
Of course, the steek can also be carefully (!) steam blocked with an iron. Once this has been achieved, leave the piece until completely dry and cool.

Then machine-secure the steek (see figure 18; sewing machine's zigzag stitch). The zigzag rows do not have to be perfect, but secure.

I recommend to place the zigzag rows between the 3rd and 4th (on the right side of the steek in figure 18) and between the 12th and 13th (on the left side of the steek in figure 18) steek stitches.

Figure 16: Kfb on the right side of the steek

Figure 17: Kfb into the 15th steek stitch

Figure 18: Zigzag stitched longitudinal seams on the right and left side of the steek

Cutting the steek

Once the steek is secured, you can cut it between the two seams (see figure 19). ▼

Figure 19: Steek cut open

The shawl now has the following measurements (see figure 20) ▼

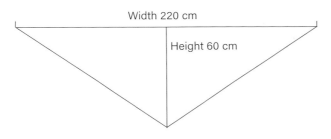

Figure 20: Dimensions after cutting the steek

These measurements are to serve as a guideline only. As mentioned before, the dimensions of your shawl can vary depending on your gauge.

Knitting the border

BC = background colours (current colour of the "magic ball")
PC = pattern colours (current colour of the "magic ball")

The border is knitted in the round and is divided into a front and back part, which will be folded together eventually - thus the steek stitches will be hidden in a kind of "pouch".

It is advisable to distribute the considerable number of stitches onto three circular needles with a cable length of at least 100 cm each (same needle size as for the body of the shawl).

Picking up stitches for the border
(See figure 21) ▼

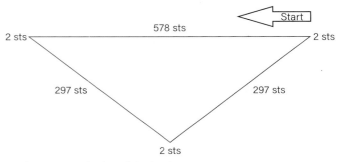

Figure 21: Beginning of the border

» K all of the top 578 sts of the shawl with BC. At the left-hand side tip of the shawl increase 1 st by kfb into the 1st "left over" stitch of the steek and place marker. This is where you will at a later stage increase and decrease stitches (see figure 22). ▼
» On the left-hand side of the shawl pick up from the line of the "1st steek sts" (see figure 22) and from the setup rows a total of 297 sts with BC.

Figure 22:
Picking up stitches for the border

» At the lower tip of the shawl (see figure 23; arrow) ▼ increase 2 sts and place 2 markers accordingly, as this is again where you will at a later stage increase and decrease stitches.
» On the right-hand side of the shawl pick up from setup rows and from the line of the "15th steek sts" a total of 297 sts with BC.
» At the right-hand side tip of the shawl (see figure 24; arrow) ▼ increase 1 st by kfb into the 15th "left over" stitch of the steek and place marker. This is where you will at a later stage increase and decrease stitches.
» Join the round.

Now you should have a total of 1,178 sts on 3 needles.

At the three tips of the shawl (2-sts-marker) please increase in each and every round 1 st each before and after the marker.

These increases are made by way of M1R and M1L (Make 1 Right and Make 1 Left).

Increase 1 st to the right of each 2-st-marker by way of M1R and increase 1 st to the left of each 2-st-marker by way of M1L.

Purl 1 row to form a small eyecatcher-line (see figure 24).

Each round will thus feature an increase of 6 sts, 1 before and 1 after the 2-st-marker at the three tips of the shawl as follows:

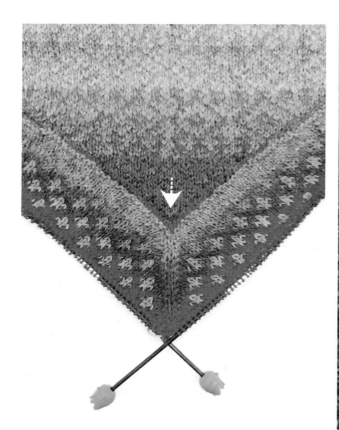

Figure 23: Lower tip of the shawl

Figure 24: Right-hand side tip of the shawl

Figure 25 / Chart 4: Border pattern

Row	24	23	22	21	20	19	18	17	16	15	14	13	12	11	10	9	8	7	6	5	4	3	2	1	Row
18	FOLDING EDGE [PURL]																								18
17																									17
16				X						X						X						X			16
15			X	X	X				X	X	X				X	X	X				X	X	X		15
14				X						X						X						X			14
13	X						X						X						X						13
12	X	X				X	X	X				X	X	X				X	X	X				X	12
11	X						X						X						X						11
10				X						X						X						X			10
9			X	X	X				X	X	X				X	X	X				X	X	X		9
8				X						X						X						X			8
7	X						X						X						X						7
6	X	X				X	X	X				X	X	X				X	X	X				X	6
5	X						X						X						X						5
4				X						X						X						X			4
3			X	X	X				X	X	X				X	X	X				X	X	X		3
2				X						X						X						X			2
1																									1

Top edge (1ˢᵗ needle)

- K 1.
- Move SM to right-hand needle.
- Inc 1 st by way of **M1L.**
- K top edge sts up to SM.
- Inc 1 st by way of **M1R.**
- Move SM to right-hand needle.
- K 1.

Left-hand edge (2ⁿᵈ needle)

- K 1.
- Move SM to right-hand needle.
- Inc 1 st by way of **M1L.**
- K left-hand edge sts up to SM.
- Inc 1 st by way of **M1R.**
- Move SM to right-hand needle.
- K 1.

Right-hand edge (3ʳᵈ needle)

- K 1.
- Move SM to right-hand needle.
- Inc 1 st by way of M1L.
- K right-hand edge sts up to SM.
- Inc 1 st by way of M1R.
- Move SM to right-hand needle.
- K 1.

= 6 sts increased in a single round.

The two stitches between the markers are always knitted in BC.

Border pattern
(See Chart 4) ▲

Rd 1: K with BC according to Chart 4.
At the three tips of the shawl (2-st-marker) inc before and after the 2-st-marker 1 st each
= total increase of 6 sts.

Rd 2 to 16: K the border pattern according to Chart 4.
Always knit the increases at the three tips of the shawl.
Due to the continuous increases, the pattern must be extended accordingly both to the right and to the left.

Rd 17: K with BC according to Chart 4.
Rd 18: Purl with BC according to Chart 4 to form the folding edge. No increases have to be knit at the three tips of the shawl.

Reverse side of the border

(see figure 26) ➤

Now all increases previously made at the three tips of the shawl border front (before and after the 2-st markers) must be decreased:

Top edge (1ˢᵗ needle)

- » K 1.
- » Move SM to right-hand needle.
- » K2tog (right-leaning decrease)
- » K top edge sts up to SM.
- » Ssk (left-leaning decrease).
- » Move SM to right-hand needle.
- » K 1.

Left-hand edge (2ⁿᵈ needle)

- » K 1.
- » Move SM to right-hand needle.
- » K2tog (right-leaning decrease)
- » K top edge sts up to SM.
- » Ssk (left-leaning decrease).
- » Move SM to right-hand needle and k 1.

Right-hand edge (3ʳᵈ needle)

- » K 1.
- » Move SM to right-hand needle.
- » K2tog (right-leaning decrease)
- » K top edge sts up to SM.
- » Ssk (left-leaning decrease).
- » Move SM to right-hand needle and k 1.

Thus 6 sts are decreased in each and every round.

For the reverse side of the border knit again all 17 rounds of the border pattern. Closely follow the pattern repeats as created for the front side of the border.

Now it is time to cast-off all stitches and sew them to the inside of the border.

It is unfortunate that sometimes the border is sewn on in a rather crooked or undulating way. In order to avoid this mistake, I would like to explain my "knit-and-sew cast-off" method in more detail.

You may want to watch the video tutorial on my Instagram account VerstrickteKunst under https://bit.ly/3QivH6j (German only).

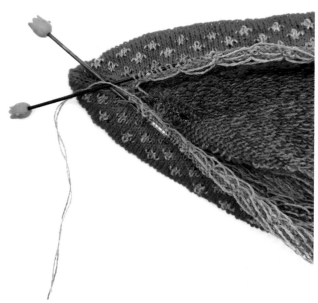

Figure 26: Reverse side of the border

"Knit-and-sew cast-off" method

(see figure 27) ▼

Figure 27: Reverse side of the border

To start, cast-off 25 sts making use of your preferred method.

Then knit the next 3 sts together with 3 sts from the border pickup row. This is done as follows:

With the help of an auxiliary needle, follow the sts down to the 1st round of the border. (see figure 28) ▼

Go into this st with the auxiliary needle.

Tilt the work so that you can see the wrong side. Next step:

Based on the position of the auxiliary needle on the 1st rd of the border, pick up the loops of 3 sts with the auxiliary needle (see figure 29). ▼

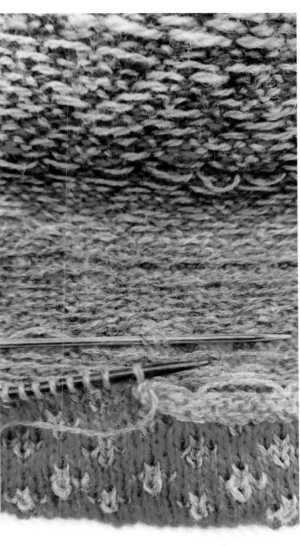

Figure 28: Auxiliary needle moved into pick-up row

Figure 29: Loops of 3 sts on the auxiliary needle

Knit the next 3 sts - one at a time! - together with one of the 3 loops picked up with the auxiliary needle and cast off (see figure 30). ▼ The steek stitches are to be encased by the double-sided border.

Then cast off the next 25 sts of the border and repeat the above steps again. The sts marked by the 2-st-marker are to be handled the same way. This results in the tips of the shawl being positioned correctly.

This technique ensures that the front and reverse sides of the shawl border will be aligned perfectly.

Sew and close the gaps that are still open and make sure to insert/hide the steek stitches inside the double-sided border (see figure 31). ▼

Figure 30: Knit together last and 1st row of the border

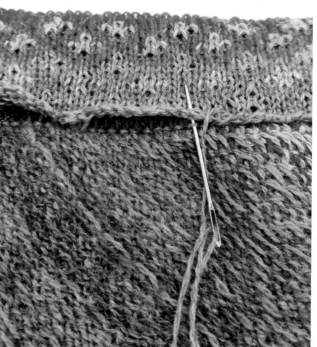

Figure 31: Sewing on the border

Once the border has been completely sewn on and all threads have been woven in, I recommend to wash and then block the shawls (see figure 32). ▼

Washing renders the single fibres softer and the knitted fabric will appear much smoother and very regular.

For this you may use your washing machine, provided it features a wool wash programme.

PLEASE BE VERY CAREFUL: It is of utmost importance (!) that the washing machine's temperature is set to cold only, as otherwise virgin/cool wool will felt! To play safe, you might also want to add a colour & dirt collector sheet/catcher, as some colours tend to bleed quite heavily, such as blue, red, and black.

All Shetland wool can be beautifully blocked: for this exercise I recommend to use blocking mats.

After washing and blocking, the shawl has the following dimensions: (see figure 33) ▼

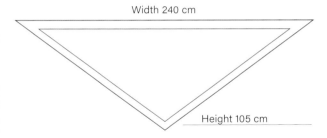

Figure 33: Dimensions of the shawl

If so desired, you might want to additionally decorate the shawl with tassels or pom-poms.

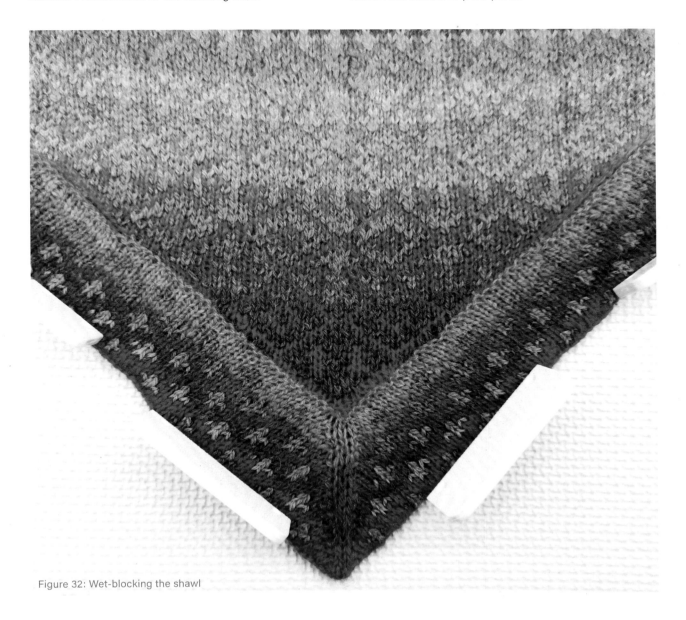

Figure 32: Wet-blocking the shawl

MAKING TASSELS AND POM-POMS

Tassels

Tassels can be made in a number of different ways.
The yarn can be wrapped around a piece of sturdy cardboard; once the yarn has been secured with a knot, the tassel can be cut open.

To create tassels, I make use of a tassel maker (see figure 34).

Tassels made with cardboard

Step 1: Wrap the yarn around a piece of sturdy cardboard. The number of wraps is determined by the intended thickness of the tassel.

Step 2: Cut a section of yarn from the skein, and pass it through the bundle as pictured, sliding it to the top and tying a knot.

Step 3: Trim the bottom of the tassel loops, to get the tassel off of the cardboard.

Step 4: Tie another section of yarn around the head of the tassel, pull tight and knot the yarn.

Step 5: Trim the bottom of all tassel strings to even them all up. Then attach the tassel to the tip of the shawl – simply use the yarn ends from tying the tassel in step 2 (above).

Figure 34: Tassel maker

Pom-Poms

I made the pom-poms with a pom-pom maker (see figure 35) Such sets are available in various sizes. I have used pom-pom makers with a diameter of 3.5 cm (Dahlias shawl), 5.5 cm (Play of the Seasons shawl, version 1) and 7.0 cm (Play of the Seasons shawl, version 2).

Of course, pom-poms can also be created with cardboard templates, that you have made yourself.

Figure 35: Pom-pom makers

Step 1:
Cut out from a piece of sturdy cardboard two identical circles with a diameter of your choice. Cut out the inner circle so that you will end up with two identical rings.

Step 2:
Place both rings on top of each other, feed the yarn through the hole and wrap it around the cardboard discs until there is no hole left in the middle.

Step 3:
Cut the yarn around the outside edge of the cardboard discs.

Step 4:
Wrap one or more pieces of yarn around the pom-pom so that they fit between the two cardboard discs. Carefully secure the pom-pom by tightly and securely tying one or more knots. You may want to use several threads of yarn in order to braid a plaited cord later.

Step 5:
Carefully remove the cardboard discs and trim the pom-pom into shape.

Step 6:
Now attach the pom-pom to the tip of the shawl - simply use the yarn ends from tying the pom-pom in step 4 (above).

Piping cord

A piping cord is formed by knitting together each and every stitch of the last round of the piping cord with the corresponding stitch of its first round. It is of importance to work exactly in the vertical line, else the piping cord might be distorted and thus lose its attractiveness.

Knit all rounds of the piping cord according to the relevant chart. From the back of the work and with an auxiliary needle, pick up the loops of all stitches of the first round (see figure 36).

Then knit together each stitch of the first round with the corresponding stitch of the last round (see figure 37). These stitches will have to remain live on your needles as they will be needed to knit the double-sided border.

Figure 36: Picking up the loops

Figure 37: Knitting together the stitches from the first and last round of the piping cord

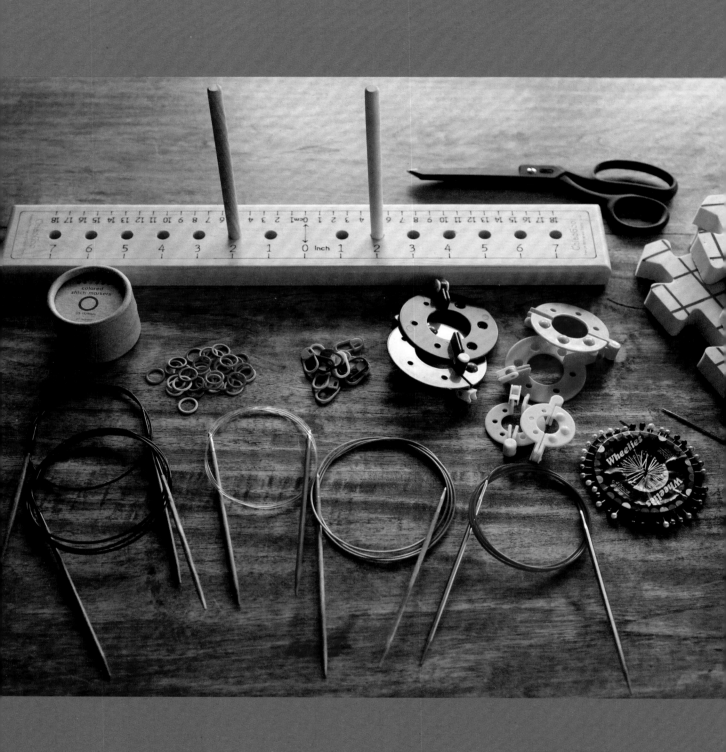

TOOLS AND NOTIONS

Knitting needles

Which knitting needle size(s) should be used depends largely on the individual gauge and swatching results. At the beginning of a shawl, the first 23 rows are generally knitted back and forth. Here you can use single pointed needles or circular needles with cable lengths between 60 and 80 cm.

As of row 24 and with the integration of steek stitches, all knitting is done in rows. Here you can start out with **double-pointed needles (DPNs)** or **circular needles** with cable length between 100 cm and 120 cm and the magic loop method.

The material of the knitting needles to choose - be they made of wood, bamboo or metal - is purely a matter of taste and depends on the individual tension of your knitted fabrics.

Stitch markers (SM)

A pattern is not only the result of individual stitches but is also determined by consecutive horizontal and vertical repeats. Horizontal repeats should be marked off with SM for better orientation. If a single repeat consists of a large number of stitches - as is the case for the *Botanico* Shawl, where a pattern repeat consists of 100 stitches - then it is recommended to split up the repeat and place SMs in different colours: you might want to place a red SM at the beginning of the repeat, a blue one in the middle and a green one each after the 25th and 75th stitch.

It is also recommended to place a SM each to point out the 1st and 15th stitch of the steek for better orientation.

Tapestry needles and pins

In order to finish the shawl, the back side of the border must be sewn on to the reverse side of the shawl. For this you will need a tapestry or darning needle. Here it is recommended to make use of the "knit-and-sew cast-off" method (see relevant chapter of the tech section) to that both sides are exactly positioned on top of each other. Pins are required to pin down the spaces in between.

Blocking mats and blocking pins

Once the shawl has been finished, it is washed and wet-blocked. Blocking mats considerably facilitate blocking and purchasing them does definitely make sense. For blocking a large shawl, you will need about 20 blocking mats each of size 30 x 30 cm. It is an investment, but it is also money well spent!

The shawl is pinned in place either with regular pins or special blocking pins, which can be purchased separately, but quite often come together with a set of blocking mats. So-called knit blockers, which resemble combs, also come in handy.

Pom-pom makers

Pom-pom makers are available in sets of various sizes. The pom-poms made for the *Play of the Seasons* Shawl have a diameter of 5.5 cm and those made for the *Dahlias* Shawl have a diameter of 3.5 cm.

Of course, pom-poms can also be created with cardboard templates, that you have made yourself.

Tassel maker

A tassel maker truly and considerably facilitates the production of tassels. I you don't want to make such a purchase you can easily produce tassels by using a strip of sturdy cardboard.

PATTERNS

FIRE LILIES

The inspiration for this shawl I got from an exhibition of Susanne Altzweig: she is a ceramic artist creating very colourful pottery and I was immediately infatuated with the combination of watercolour and terracotta shades.

Yarn

Abbreviation	Yarn Manufacturer	Yardage/100g
G	Gardiner S08 Shetland (100% wool)	450m/100g
G1	Gardiner SS11 Soft Shetland (100% wool)	565m/100g
H	Harrisville New England Shetland (100% pure wool)	397m/100g
J	Jamieson of Shetland Shetland Spindrift (100% pure Shetland wool)	420m/100g
JU	Jamieson of Shetland Ultra (50% Shetland/50% lambswool)	776m/100g
K	Knoll Supersoft (100% PURE NEW WOOL)	576m/100g
SF	Lankava Esito worsted wool yarn (100% wool)	425m/100g
Ra	Rauma F inull PT2 (100% Norwegian wool)	350m/100g
Re	Rennie Supersoft (100% lambswool)	565m/100g
ReU	Rennie Unique Shetland (100% lambswool)	450m/100g
ReC	Rennie Supersoft Cashmere (87.5% lambswool/12.5% cashmere)	492m/100g
LT	Tines 100% wool	350m/100g

Shetland Spindrift, Supersoft (lambswool), pure new wool etc. The yardage of the different yarns varies. Further information can be found in the chapter concerning yarns and suppliers (see pp. 160-161).

Version 1 "Turquoise + Terracotta"

Yarn kit "Fire Lilies - Version 1" as available from Bärbel Salet VerstrickteKunst or

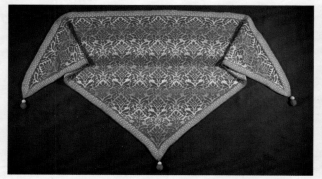

370 g pattern colour(s) (PC)
8 x 40 g Poppy (J), Saffron (K), Ember (K), Iron Rust (Re), Spice (Re), Lelantos (ReC), Poppy (H), Brandy (K)
1 x 50 g Ginger (J)

300 g background colour(s) (BC)
10 x 30 g Aquamarine (K), Marble Gemstone (Re), Seagreen (H), Mint Julip (JU), Shamrock Shake (Re), Ice Water (G), Iced (K), Porcelain (ReU), Mineral Blue (G), Seabright (J)

140 g Aquamarine (K) for the border (BC)

The amount of yarn required for the pom-poms is included in the above.

Version 2 "Mustard Yellow + Red Orange Pink Berry"

Yarn kit "Fire Lilies - Version 2" as available from Bärbel Salet VerstrickteKunst or

430 g pattern colour(s) (PC)
19 x 20 g Peony (K), Carnation (Re), Raspberry (H), Plum (J), Grenadine (Re), Poppy (K), Queen of Hearts (G), Scarlet (H), Tudor (Re), Scarlet (Re), Poppy (H), Lelantos (ReC), Spice (Re), Pumpkin (J), #760 Papaya (LT), Jaffa (Re), Flame (J), Geranium (K), Red Clover (K)
1 x 50 g Pink (H)

380 g background colour(s) (BC)
4 x 75 g Cornfield (J), Mustard (J), Yellow Ochre (J), Broom (G)
1 x 80 g Mustard (H)

The amount of yarn required for the border and the tassels/pom-poms is included in the above.

Chart 1

23		(43 sts)	+					x	x	x	x				x	x	x		x	x	x		x	x	x		x	x	x		x	x	x			x	x	x	x				o		RS	23
22	WS			o	x	x		x	x	x						x				x			x			x			x									x	x	x		x	x	+	A	(41 sts)		22
21		(39 sts)	A	+	x	x		x	x	x				x	x	x	x			x	x				x	x								x	x	x	x		x	x	x	o				RS	21
20	WS				o	x	x		x	x		x	x	x	x	x	x		x	x		x	x				x	x		x	x	x	x	x	x			x	x		x	x	+	A	(37 sts)		20
19		(35 sts)		A	+	x		x	x		x	x	x	x		x	x	x	x	x		x	x			x	x	x			x	x	x	x	x			x	x		x	o				RS	19
18	WS					o	x		x	x			x	x			x	x	x	x	x			x	x	x				x	x	x	x	x	x			x	x		x	+	A		(33 sts)		18
17		(31 sts)			A	+		x	x			x	x			x	x	x	x	x			x	x	x				x	x	x	x	x				x	x		o					RS	17
16	WS						o		x			x	x	x	x	x			x	x	x			x	x	x	x	x					x				x		+	A			(29 sts)		16
15		(27 sts)				A	+					x	x			x	x			x	x			x	x							o											RS	15
14	WS						o					x				x					x						x					+	A							(25 sts)		14
13		(23 sts)					A	+			x	x	x	x	x			x	x	x	x	x						o															RS	13
12	WS							o		x	x	x			x	x	x		x	x	x						+	A													(21 sts)		12
11		(19 sts)						A	+		x	x	x	x		x	x	x	x				o																				RS	11
10	WS								o		x	x	x		x		x	x	x			+	A																		(17 sts)		10
9		(15 sts)							A	+			x			x				o																						RS	9
8	WS									o			x	x	x			+	A																					(13 sts)		8
7		(11 sts)							A	+		x	x	x			o																									RS	7
6	WS								o			x			+	A																								(9 sts)		6
5		(7 sts)						A	+		x		o																												RS	5
4	WS							o			A																												(5 sts)		4
3		(4 sts)						A		o																															RS	3
2	WS							A																																		2
1									|	|	|																															RS	1

43 42 41 40 39 38 37 36 35 34 33 32 31 30 29 28 27 26 25 24 23 22 21 20 19 18 17 16 15 14 13 12 11 10 9 8 7 6 5 4 3 2 1

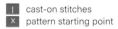

Chart 1

Symbol	Meaning	Symbol	Meaning	Symbol	Meaning
x	pattern colour(s)	|	cast-on stitches	A	chain cast-on stitch
(shaded)	background colour(s)	x (shaded)	pattern starting point	o	knit
				+	purl bump increase

RS right side row
WS wrong side row

Arrangement of colours

The gradient colour schemes of both PC and BC are achieved with the help of previously prepared "magic balls", see the technical chapter, p. 13 ff. The wingspans are being determined individually.

Needles

3.25 mm circular needles (with different cable lengths); adjust needle size to obtain gauge if necessary.
DPNs might be useful at the beginning of the shawl.
3 sets of 3.25 mm circular needles with 100 cm cables for knitting the border; adjust needle size to obtain gauge if necessary.

Gauge

27 sts and 32 rows with 3.25 mm needles = 10 x 10 cm

Dimensions

Width 235 cm
Height 102 cm

Stitches

Stockinette stitch; two-colour Fair Isle knitting

Starting the shawl

R 1 cast-on row: co 3 sts with BC [|]
R 2 (WS): p 3 + chain cast-on 1 st [A]
R 3 (RS): k [o], k 3 sts = 4 sts, chain cast-on 1 st [A]
R 4 (WS): k [o], p 4 sts = 5 sts, chain cast-on 1 st [A]
R 5 (RS): This row marks the beginning/starting point of the patterned section. From this row onwards 1 st is increased each at the beginning [A] and at the end [+].
K R 6 (WS) up to and including R 23 (RS).

Integration of steek stitches

R 23 (RS/43 sts on needle): At the end of this row chain cast-on 15 steek sts, alternating between BC and PC. Close the row to a round.
Continue knitting either with DPNs or using the Magic Loop technique.

Please change to Chart 2 / R 24.

First round with steek stitches

Start knitting R 24 with the following partition (Chart 2):
» K from st 9 up to and including st 51. Place SM.
» K 14 steek sts according to the established colour scheme. Place SM.
» K the 15th steek st.

This first round with steek stitches does not feature any increase.

From R 25 onwards and all following rounds

» K all sts according to Chart 2/R 25.
» At the end of this R, inc 1 st by kfb from the last st.
» Move SM to the right needle.
» K 14 steek sts.
» Move SM to the right needle.
» Inc 1 st by kfb from the 15th steek stitch

As increases are regularly added, the pattern must also be extended to the right and left. For better orientation, completed horizontal pattern repeats should be identified by the placement of SMs.

Chart 2

43

Chart 3

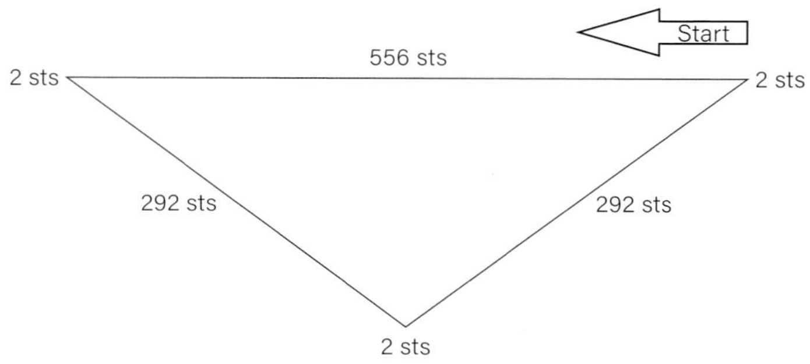

Start

2 sts — 556 sts — 2 sts

292 sts   292 sts

2 sts

Version 1
BC = Aquamarine (K)
PC = see Chart 4

Version 2
BC = mustard yellow "magic ball"
PC = see Chart 4

Once the first pattern repeat has been achieved hight-wise, start again with R 1.

In the end the shawl will be 281 rounds high (4 x 60 R of the complete pattern repeat plus one partial repeat from R 1 to and including R 41) and 556 sts wide.

The pattern is repeated 9 times horizontally in total (9 x 60 sts = 540 sts) plus the first 8 sts of a pattern repeat on the upper left tip and the last 8 sts of a pattern repeat on the upper right tip. = 556 sts

Cutting the steek

Bind off steek sts 2 until 14 inclusive. Moisten and block the steek. When dry, secure the steek and cut it open.

	18	17	16	15	14	13	12	11	10	9	8	7	6	5	4	3	2	1	PC [x] Version 1	PC [x] Version 2	
34																					34
33					x	x					x	x					x	x	Seabright (J)	Flame (J)	33
32					x	x					x	x					x	x	Seabright (J)	Flame (J)	32
31		x	x					x	x					x	x				Marble Gemstone (Re)	Jaffa (Re)	31
30		x	x					x	x					x	x				Marble Gemstone (Re)	Jaffa (Re)	30
29					x	x					x	x					x	x	Seagreen (H)	#760 Papaya (LT)	29
28					x	x					x	x					x	x	Seagreen (H)	#760 Papaya (LT)	28
27		x	x					x	x					x	x				Mint Julip (JU)	Pumpkin (J)	27
26		x	x					x	x					x	x				Mint Julip (JU)	Pumpkin (J)	26
25					x	x					x	x					x	x	Shamrock Shake (Re)	Spice (Re)	25
24					x	x					x	x					x	x	Shamrock Shake (Re)	Spice (Re)	24
23		x	x					x	x					x	x				Iced (K)	Lelantos (ReC)	23
22		x	x					x	x					x	x				Iced (K)	Lelantos (ReC)	22
21					x	x					x	x					x	x	Porcelain (ReU)	Poppy (H)	21
20					x	x					x	x					x	x	Porcelain (ReU)	Poppy (H)	20
19																					19
18					F O L D I N G E D G E [P U R L]														Ginger (J) only	Pink (H) only	18
17																			Ginger (J) only	Pink (H) only	17
16																					16
15					x	x					x	x					x	x	Seabright (J)	Scarlet (Re)	15
14					x	x					x	x					x	x	Seabright (J)	Scarlet (Re)	14
13		x	x					x	x					x	x				Marble Gemstone (Re)	Tudor (Re)	13
12		x	x					x	x					x	x				Marble Gemstone (Re)	Tudor (Re)	12
11					x	x					x	x					x	x	Seagreen (H)	Queen (K)	11
10					x	x					x	x					x	x	Seagreen (H)	Queen (K)	10
9		x	x					x	x					x	x				Mint Julip (JU)	Poppy (K)	9
8		x	x					x	x					x	x				Mint Julip (JU)	Poppy (K)	8
7					x	x					x	x					x	x	Shamrock Shake (Re)	Grenadine (Re)	7
6					x	x					x	x					x	x	Shamrock Shake (Re)	Grenadine (Re)	6
5		x	x					x	x					x	x				Iced (K)	Plum (J)	5
4		x	x					x	x					x	x				Iced (K)	Plum (J)	4
3					x	x					x	x					x	x	Porcelain (ReU)	Raspberry (H)	3
2					x	x					x	x					x	x	Porcelain (ReU)	Raspberry (H)	2
1																					1
	18	17	16	15	14	13	12	11	10	9	8	7	6	5	4	3	2	1			

Chart 4

Border

K all 556 sts of the upper edge with Ginger (J) for Version 1 or Pink (H) for Version 2.

Inc 1 st by kfb from the 1st steek st and place SM (left tip; 2-st-marker).
Pick up and knit 292 sts on the left side.
At the bottom tip inc 2 sts and place SM (2-st-marker).
Pick up and knit 292 sts on the right side.

Inc 1 st by kfb from the 15th steek st and place SM (right tip; 2-st-marker).
Purl one rd with Ginger (J) for Version 1 or Pink (H) for Version 2 (eyecatcher line).
At each of the 2-st-markers inc 1 st on both sides by M1R and M1L

Each round will thus feature an increase of 6 sts.

BORDER PATTERN

R 1: k with BC.

The sts of the 2-st-markers are always knitted with BC.

The PC colour arrangement for the border [x] is mentioned in the right-hand side columns of Chart 4.

Please be reminded to regularly increase (2-st-markers) at all three tips of the shawl. Due to the continuous increases, the pattern must also be extended to the left and the right.

R 2-15: k the border pattern with BC and PC according to Chart 4.
R 16: k with BC only.
R 17: k with the yarn colour according to Chart 4.
R 18: p with the yarn colour according to Chart 4 (folding edge). No increases are knitted at the three tips of the shawl.

Reverse side of the border

Now all increases previously made at the three tips of the shawl border front (2-st markers) must be decreased.

In each R before and after the 2-st-marker 1 st each has to be decreased left-leaning (ssk) and right-leaning (k2tog) accordingly.

This way 6 sts are being decreased in each round.

Please follow the pattern repeats as created for the front side of the border.
R 19: k with BC only.

R 20-33: k the border pattern with PC according to Chart 4.
R 34: k with BC only.

Cast-off all sts and sew them to the inside of the border. See the description of the "knit-and-sew cast-off" method (see pp. 24-26)

Finishing the shawl

Wash and block the shawl.
After drying the shawl, you might want to prepare tassels/pom-poms and sew them to the tips of the shawl.

GINKGO

I got the inspiration for this shawl from nature.
Ginkgo trees are glowing in so many beautiful colours - and the
shape of its leaves inspired me to create this pattern.

Yarn

Abbreviation	Yarn Manufacturer	Yardage/100g
G	Gardiner S08 Shetland (100% Wool)	450m/100g
G1	Gardiner SS11 Soft Shetland (100% Wool)	565m/100g
H	Harrisville New England Shetland (100% pure wool)	397m/100g
J	Jamieson of Shetland Shetland Spindrift (100% pure Shetland wool)	420m/100g
JU	Jamieson of Shetland Ultra (50% Shetland/50% lambswool)	776m/100g
K	Knoll Supersoft (100% PURE NEW WOOL)	576m/100g
SF	Lankava Esito worsted wool yarn (100% wool)	425m/100g
Ra	Rauma Finull PT2 (100% Norwegian wool)	350m/100g
Re	Rennie Supersoft (100% lambswool)	565m/100g
ReU	Rennie Unique Shetland (100% lambswool)	450m/100g
ReC	Rennie Supersoft Cashmere (87.5% lambswool/12.5% cashmere)	492m/100g
LT	Tines 100% wool	350m/100g

Shetland Spindrift, Supersoft (lambswool), pure new wool etc. The yardage of the different yarns varies. Further information can be found in the chapter concerning yarns and suppliers (see pp. 160-161).

Version 1 "Pink-Berry + Yellow-Lime-Leafy Green"

Yarn kit "Ginkgo - Version 1" as available from Bärbel Salet VerstrickteKunst or

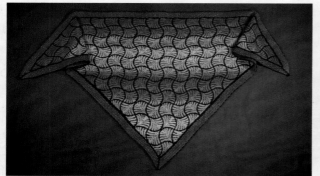

320 g pattern colour(s) (PC)
8 x 40 g Lime (J), #454 Lime Green (Ra), #340 Lime (LT), Stonehenge (Re), Lime (H), #8036 Light Green (SF), #8040 Leaf Green (SF), Apple (J)

300 g background colour(s) (BC)
10 x 30 g Amaranth Mix (Re), Magenta (H), Petunia (Re), Elderberry (G), Raspberry (H), Plum (J), Lavish (Re), Chianti (H), Mantilla (J), Imperial Purple (K)

100 g Plum (J) for the border (BC)
100 g Mantilla (J) for the border (PC)

Version 2 "Mocha + Autumn Shades"

Yarn kit "Ginkgo - Version 2" as available from Bärbel Salet VerstrickteKunst or

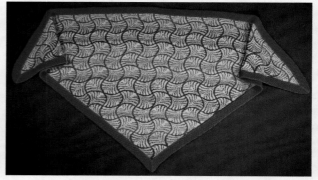

320 g pattern colour(s) (PC)
16 x 15 g Foliage (H), Goldcrest (K), Yellow Ochre (J), Mustard (H), Broom (G), Goldenrod (H), Mustard (J), Cornfield (J), #740 Orange (LT), Hephaestus (ReC), Jaffa (Re), Spice (Re), Lelantos (ReC), Saffron (K), Iron Rust (Re), Ember (K)
4 x 20 g Topaz (H), Paprika (J), #760 Papaya (LT), Pumpkin (J)

380 g background colour(s) (BC)
Mocha (G)

100 g Mocha (G) for border (BC)
100 g Iron Rust (Re) for border (PC)

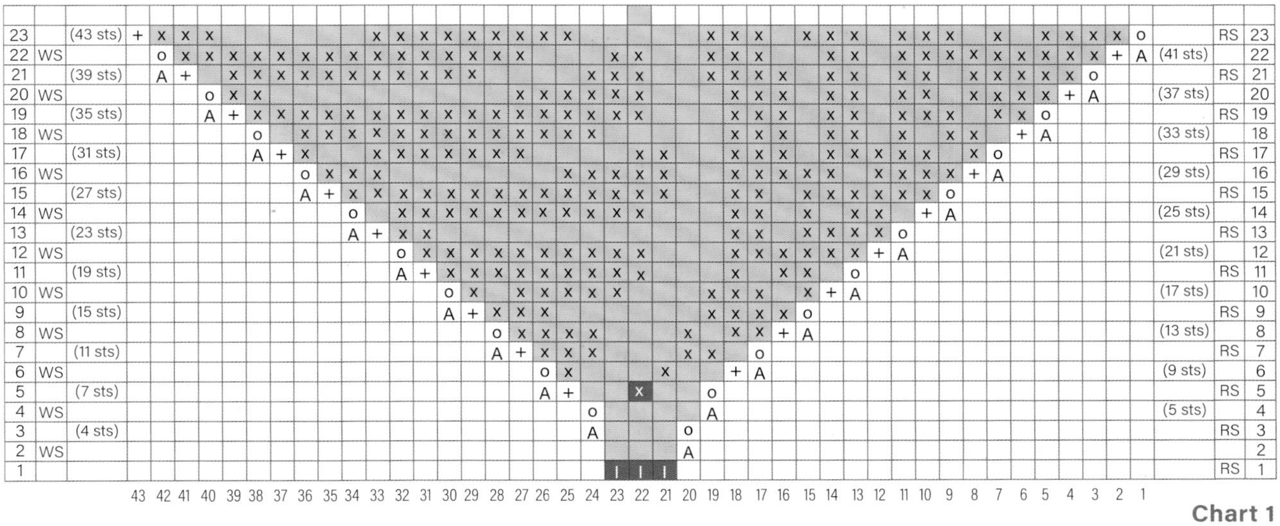

Chart 1

- [x] pattern colour(s)
- [ ] background colour(s)
- [I] cast-on stitches
- [x] pattern starting point
- [A] chain cast-on stitch
- [o] knit
- [+] purl bump increase
- RS right side row
- WS wrong side row

Arrangement of colours

Version 1

The gradient colour schemes of both PC and BC are achieved with the help of previously prepared "magic balls", see the technical chapter, p. 13 ff. The wingspans are being determined individually.

Version 2

The PC colour scheme is knitted according to a pre-determined number of rows per colour.

In order to obtain a two-fold repetition for the altogether 20 colours of the shawl, each colour was knitted for 7 and 8 rounds in rotation; please cf. a sample calculation in the technical chapter (see p. 13).

Needles

3.25 mm circular needles (with different cable lengths); adjust needle size to obtain gauge if necessary.

DPNs might be useful at the beginning of the shawl.

3 sets of 3.25 mm circular needles with 100 cm cables for knitting the border; adjust needle size to obtain gauge if necessary.

Gauge

27 sts and 32 rows with 3.25 mm needles = 10 x 10 cm

Dimensions

Width 239 cm

Height 104 cm

Stitches

Stockinette stitch; two-colour fair isle knitting

Starting the shawl

R 1 cast-on row: co 3 sts with BC [|]

R 2 (WS): p 3 + chain cast-on 1 st [A]

R 3 (RS): k [o], k 3 sts = 4 sts, chain cast-on 1 st [A]

R 4 (WS): k [o], p 4 sts = 5 sts, chain cast-on 1 st [A]

R 5 (RS): This row marks the beginning/starting point of the patterned section.

From this row onwards 1 st is increased each at the beginning [A] and at the end [+].

K R 6 (WS) up to and including R 23 (RS).

Integration of steek stitches

R 23 (RS/43 sts on needle): At the end of this row chain cast-on 15 steek sts, alternating between BC and PC. Close the row to a round. From now on all rows are k only. Continue knitting either with DPNs or using the Magic Loop technique.

Please change to Chart 2 / R 24.

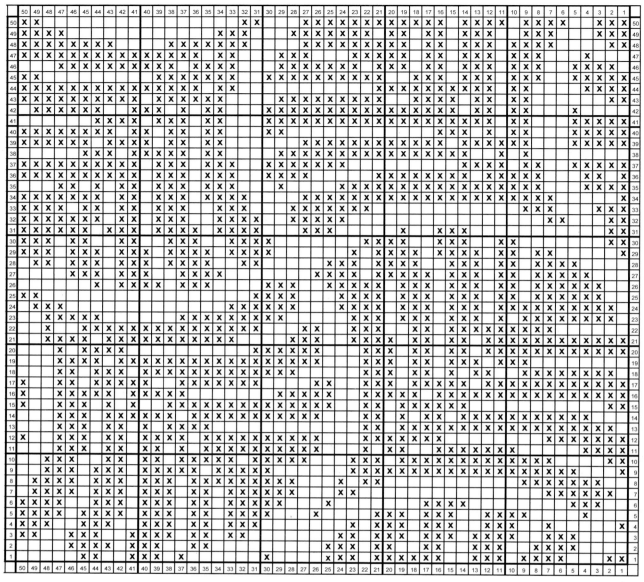

Chart 2

First round with steek stitches

Start knitting R 24 with the following partition (Chart 2):

» K from st 5 up to and including st 47.
» Place SM.
» K 14 steek sts according to the established colour scheme.
» Place SM.
» K the 15th steek st.

This first round with steek stitches does not feature any increase.

From R 25 onwards and all following rounds

» K all sts according to Chart 2/R 25.
» At the end of this R, inc 1 st by kfb from the last st.
» Move SM to the right needle.
» K 14 steek sts.
» Move SM to the right needle.
» Inc 1 st by kfb from the 15th steek stitch

As increases are regularly added, please also extend the pattern accordingly.

Chart 3

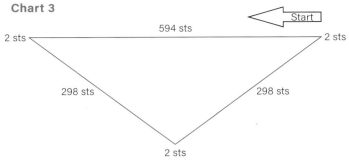

2 sts — 594 sts — Start — 2 sts

298 sts — 298 sts

2 sts

Version 1
BC = Plum (J)
PC = Mantilla (J)

Version 2
BC = Mocha (G)
PC = Iron Rust (E)

For better orientation, completed horizontal pattern repeats should be identified by the placement of SMs. Once the first pattern repeat has been achieved height-wise, start again with R 1.

In the end the shawl will be 300 rounds high (6 x 50 R of the complete pattern) and 594 sts wide.

The pattern is repeated 11 times horizontally in total (11 x 50 sts = 550 sts) plus the first 22 sts of a pattern repeat on the upper left tip and the last 22 sts of a pattern repeat on the upper right tip.
= 594 sts

Cutting the steek
Bind off steek sts 2 until 14 inclusive. Moisten and block the steek. When dry, secure the steek and cut it open.

Border
K all 594 sts of the upper edge with Plum (J) for Version 1 or Mocha (G) for Version 2.

Inc 1 st by kfb from the 1st steek st and place SM (left tip; 2-st-marker).
Pick up and knit 298 sts on the left side.
At the bottom tip inc 2 sts and place SM (2-st-marker).
Pick up and knit 298 sts on the right side.

Inc 1 st by kfb from the 15th steek st and place SM (right tip; 2-st-marker).

Purl one rd with Plum (J) for Version 1 or Mocha (G) for Version 2 (eyecatcher line).

At each of the 2-st-markers inc 1 st on both sides by M1R and M1L

Each round will thus feature an increase of 6 sts.

BORDER PATTERN

R	16	15	14	13	12	11	10	9	8	7	6	5	4	3	2	1	R
19	F	O	L	D	I	N	G		E	D	G	E					19
18																	18
17	x	x	x	x					x	x	x	x					17
16	x			x		x	x		x			x		x	x		16
15	x			x		x	x		x			x		x	x		15
14	x	x	x	x					x	x	x	x					14
13					x	x	x	x					x	x	x	x	13
12		x	x		x			x		x	x		x			x	12
11		x	x		x			x		x	x		x			x	11
10					x	x	x	x					x	x	x	x	10
9	x	x	x	x					x	x	x	x					9
8	x			x		x	x		x			x		x	x		8
7	x			x		x	x		x			x		x	x		7
6	x	x	x	x					x	x	x	x					6
5					x	x	x	x					x	x	x	x	5
4		x	x		x			x		x	x		x			x	4
3		x	x		x			x		x	x		x			x	3
2					x	x	x	x					x	x	x	x	2
1																	1
	16	15	14	13	12	11	10	9	8	7	6	5	4	3	2	1	

Chart 4

R 1: k with BC.

The sts of the 2-st-markers are always knitted with BC.

Please be reminded to regularly increase (2-st-markers) at all three tips of the shawl.

R 2-17: k the border pattern with BC and PC according to Chart 4.
R 18: k with BC only.
R 19: p with BC (folding edge). No increases are knitted at the three tips of the shawl.

Reverse side of the border

Now all increases previously made at the three tips of the shawl border front (2-st markers) must be decreased.

In each R before and after the 2-st-marker 1 st each has to be decreased left-leaning (ssk) and right-leaning (k2tog) accordingly.
This way 6 sts are being decreased in each round.

Please follow the pattern repeats as created for the front side of the border.

K R 18 up to R 1 of the border pattern for the reverse side of the border.

Cast-off all sts and sew them to the inside of the border. See the description of the "knit-and-sew cast-off" method (see pp. 24-26)

Finishing the shawl
Wash and block the shawl.

Optional: After drying the shawl, you might want to prepare tassels/pom-poms and sew them to the tips of the shawl.

Fan Flowers

The colour combination of purple and orange had been on my mind
for a long time and I also found very beautiful photos on Pinterest.
I was particularly impressed by an American wedding.
The bridesmaids wore purple dresses and carried matching
bouquets of orange-coloured flowers. Wow!

Yarn

Abbreviation	Yarn Manufacturer	Yardage/100g
G	Gardiner S08 Shetland (100% wool)	450m/100g
G1	Gardiner SS11 Soft Shetland (100% wool)	565m/100g
H	Harrisville New England Shetland (100% pure Wool)	397m/100g
J	Jamieson of Shetland Shetland Spindrift (100% pure Shetland wool)	420m/100g
JU	Jamieson of Shetland Ultra (50% Shetland/50% lambswool)	776m/100g
K	Knoll Supersoft (100% PURE NEW WOOL)	576m/100g
SF	Lankava Esito worsted wool yarn (100% wool)	425m/100g
Ra	Rauma Finull PT2 (100% Norwegian wool)	350m/100g
Re	Rennie Supersoft (100% lambswool)	565m/100g
ReU	Rennie Unique Shetland (100% lambswool)	450m/100g
ReC	Rennie Supersoft Cashmere (87.5% lambswool/12.5% cashmere)	492m/100g
LT	Tines 100% wool	350m/100g

Shetland Spindrift, Supersoft (lambswool), pure new wool etc. The yardage of the different yarns varies. Further information can be found in the chapter concerning yarns and suppliers (see pp. 160-161).

Version 1 "Purple + Orange"

Yarn kit "Fan Flowers - Version 1" as available from Bärbel Salet VerstrickteKunst or

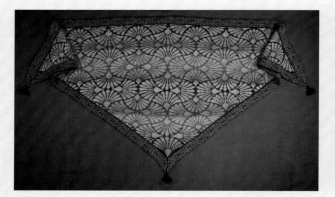

315 g pattern colour(s) (PC)

7 x 45 g #740 Orange (LT), Clementine (K), #8025 Orange (SF), Pumpkin (J), #760 Papaya (LT), Jaffa (Re), Spice (Re)

230 g background colour(s) (BC)

10 x 23 g Blackberry (H), Clover (J), Zodiac (J), Orchid (K), Violet (H), Purple (J), Delphinium (H), Ivanhoe (Re), Blueberry (Re), Mulberry (J)

150 g Blueberry (Re) for border (BC)
120 g New Amethyst (Re) for border (PC)

Version 2 "Petrol-Dark Blue + Pink-Berry"

Yarn kit "Fan Flowers - Version 2" as available from Bärbel Salet VerstrickteKunst or

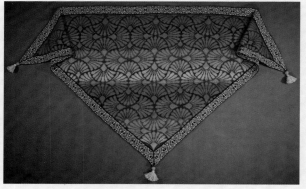

310 g pattern colour(s) (PC)

6 x 25 g Peony (K), Carnation (Re), Plum (J), Lavish (Re), Elderberry (G), Loganberry (K)
3 x 30 g Pink (H), Raspberry (H), Magenta (H)
2 x 35 g Chianti (H), Cherry (J)

230 g background colour(s) (BC)

4 x 25 g Denim (Re), Indigo (K), Mariner (K), Petrel (Re)
2 x 30 g Loden Blue (H), Petrel (G),
2 x 35 g Midnight (G), Vintage Heather (K)

150 g Midnight (G) for border (BC)
120 g Aquamarine (K) for border (PC)

Version 2 | BC colour arrangement

1st Cycle
Rows 1 to 18 – Denim (Re)
Rows 19 to 36 – Indigo (K)
Rows 37 to 54 – Mariner (K)
Rows 55 to 72 – Loden Blue
Rows 73 to 90 – Petrel (Re)
Rows 91 to 100 – Petrel (G)

2nd Cycle
Rows 1 to 9 – Petrel (G)
Rows 10 to 26 – Midnight (G)
Rows 27 to 44 – Vintage Heather (K)
Rows 45 to 62 – Denim (Re)
Rows 63 to 80 – Indigo (K)
Rows 81 to 98 – Mariner (K)
Rows 99 to 100 – Loden Blue (H)

3rd Cycle
Rows 1 to 16 – Loden Blue (H)
Rows 17 to 34 – Petrel (Re)
Rows 35 to 52 – Petrel (G)
Rows 53 to 70 – Midnight (G)
Rows 71 to 87 – Vintage Heather (K)
Rows 88 to 97 – Denim (Re)

Version 2 | PC colour arrangement

1st Cycle
Rows 5 to 17 – Peony (K)
Rows 18 to 30 – Carnation (Re)
Rows 31 to 43 – Pink (H)
Rows 44 to 56 – Plum (J)
Rows 57 to 69 – Raspberry (H)
Rows 70 to 82 – Lavish (Re)
Rows 83 to 95 – Elderberry (G)
Rows 96 to 100 – Magenta (H)

2nd Cycle
Rows 1 to 8 – Magenta (H)
Rows 9 to 21 – Amaranth Mix (Re)
Rows 22 to 31 – Chianti (H)
Rows 32 to 40 – Cherry (J)
Rows 41 to 47 – Lavish (Re)
Rows 48 to 52 – Raspberry (H)
Rows 53 to 65 – Peony (K)
Rows 66 to 78 – Carnation (Re)
Rows 79 to 91 – Pink (H)
Rows 92 to 100 – Plum (J)

3rd Cycle
Row 1 to 4 – Plum (J)
Row 5 to 17 – Raspberry (H)
Row 18 to 30 – Lavish (Re)
Row 31 to 43 – Elderberry (G)
Row 44 to 56 – Magenta (H)
Row 57 to 69 – Amaranth Mix (Re)
Row 70 to 82 – Chianti (H)
Row 83 to 97 – Cherry (J)

Arrangement of colours

Version 1
The gradient colour schemes of both PC and BC are achieved with the help of previously prepared "magic balls", see the technical chapter, p. 13 ff. The wingspans are being determined individually.

Version 2
Both PC and BC colour schemes are knitted according to a predetermined number of rows per colour.

Needles
3.25 mm circular needles (with different cable lengths); adjust needle size to obtain gauge if necessary. DPNs might be useful at the beginning of the shawl.

3 sets of 3.25 mm circular needles with 100 cm cables for knitting the border; adjust needle size to obtain gauge if necessary.

Gauge
27 sts and 32 rows with 3.25 mm needles = 10 x 10 cm

Dimensions
Width 239 cm
Height 107 cm

Stitches
Stockinette stitch; two-colour Fair Isle knitting

Starting the shawl
R 1 cast-on row: co 3 sts with BC [|]
R 2 (WS): p 3 + chain cast-on 1 st [A]
R 3 (RS): k [o], k 3 sts = 4 sts, chain cast-on 1 st [A]
R 4 (WS): k [o], p 4 sts = 5 sts, chain cast-on 1 st [A]
R 5 (RS): This row marks the beginning/starting point of the patterned section. From this row onwards 1 st is increased each at the beginning [A] and at the end [+].
K R 6 (WS) up to and including R 23 (RS).

Integration of steek stitches
R 23 (RS/43 sts on needle): At the end of this row chain cast-on 15 steek sts, alternating between BC and PC.
Close the row to a round. From now on, the shawl is knit in the round in stockinette st.
Continue knitting either with DPNs or using the Magic Loop technique

Please change to Chart 2 / R 24.

First round with steek stitches
Start knitting R 24 with the following partition (Chart 2):
» K from st 9 up to and including st 51. Place SM.
» K 14 steek sts according to the established colour scheme. Place SM.
» K the 15th steek st.

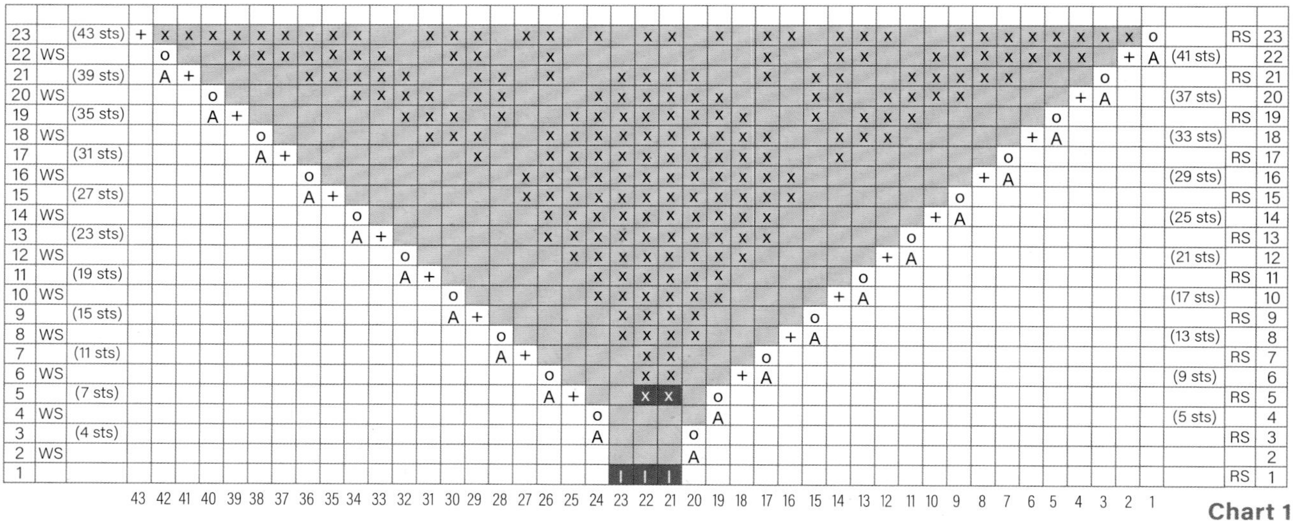

Chart 1

Column numbers (right to left): 43 42 41 40 39 38 37 36 35 34 33 32 31 30 29 28 27 26 25 24 23 22 21 20 19 18 17 16 15 14 13 12 11 10 9 8 7 6 5 4 3 2 1

Row	side	sts (left)	sts (right)	side	Row
23		(43 sts)		RS	23
22	WS		(41 sts)		22
21		(39 sts)		RS	21
20	WS		(37 sts)		20
19		(35 sts)		RS	19
18	WS		(33 sts)		18
17		(31 sts)		RS	17
16	WS		(29 sts)		16
15		(27 sts)		RS	15
14	WS		(25 sts)		14
13		(23 sts)		RS	13
12	WS		(21 sts)		12
11		(19 sts)		RS	11
10	WS		(17 sts)		10
9		(15 sts)		RS	9
8	WS		(13 sts)		8
7		(11 sts)		RS	7
6	WS		(9 sts)		6
5		(7 sts)		RS	5
4	WS		(5 sts)		4
3		(4 sts)		RS	3
2	WS				2
1				RS	1

Legend

Symbol	Meaning	Symbol	Meaning
x (shaded)	pattern colour(s)	A	chain cast-on stitch
(grey)	background colour(s)	o	knit
I	cast-on stitches	+	purl bump increase
x (black)	pattern starting point	RS	right side row
		WS	wrong side row

This first round with steek stitches does not feature any increase.

From R 25 onwards and all following rounds

» K all sts according to Chart 2/R 25.
» At the end of this R, inc 1 st by kfb from the last st.
» Move SM to the right needle.
» K 14 steek sts.
» Move SM to the right needle.
» Inc 1 st by kfb from the 15th steek stitch

As increases are regularly added, the pattern must also be extended to the right and left.

For better orientation, completed horizontal pattern repeats should be identified by the placement of SMs. Once the first pattern repeat has been achieved hight-wise, start again with R 1.

In the end the shawl will be 297 rounds high (2 x 100 R of the complete pattern repeat plus one partial repeat from R 1 to and including R 97) and 588 sts wide.

The pattern is repeated 5 times horizontally in total (5 x 96 sts = 480 sts) plus the first 54 sts of a pattern repeat on the upper left tip and the last 54 sts of a pattern repeat on the upper right tip = 588 sts.

Cutting the steek

Bind off steek sts 2 until 14 inclusive. Moisten and block the steek. When dry, secure the steek and cut it open.

Border

K all 588 sts of the upper edge with Blueberry (J) for Version 1 or Aquamarine (K) for Version 2.

Inc 1 st by kfb from the 1st steek st and place SM (left tip; 2-st-marker).
Pick up and knit 308 sts on the left side.
At the bottom tip inc 2 sts and place SM (2-st-marker).
Pick up and knit 308 sts on the right side.

Inc 1 st by kfb from the 15th steek st and place SM (right tip; 2-st-marker).

Purl one rd with Blueberry (J) for Version 1 or Midnight (&) for Version 2 (eyecatcher line).

At each of the 2-st-markers inc 1 st on both sides by M1R and M1L

Each round will thus feature an increase of 6 sts.

BORDER PATTERN

R 1: k with BC. The sts of the 2-st-markers are always knitted with BC.

Please be reminded to regularly increase (2-st-markers) at all three tips of the shawl. Due to the continuous increases, the pattern must also be extended to the left and the right.

R 2: The sts at the top row (588 sts + 2 x (LFT + RT) inc 2 sts = 592 sts) are to be arranged as follows:
» k 1 x the last 6 sts of Chart 4 with BC and PC according to Chart 4.

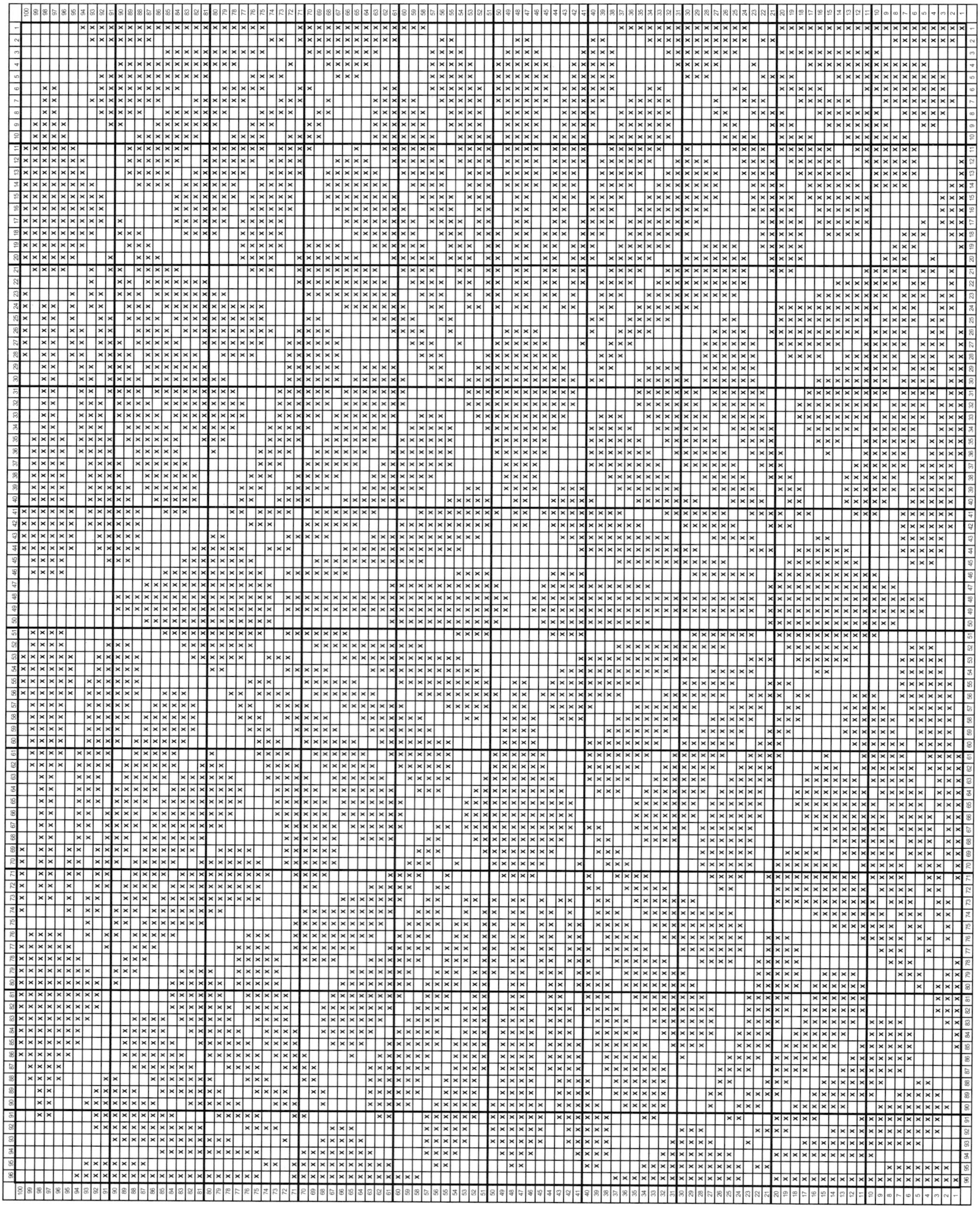

Chart 2

Chart 3

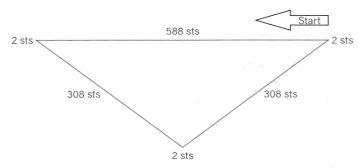

Start

588 sts

2 sts · 2 sts

308 sts · 308 sts

2 sts

Version 1
BC = Blueberry (Re)
PC = New Amethyst (Re)

Version 2
BC = Midnight (G)
PC = Aquamarine (K)

	20	19	18	17	16	15	14	13	12	11	10	9	8	7	6	5	4	3	2	1	
24		F	O	L	D	I	N	G		E	D	G	E		[P	U	R	L]			24
23																					23
22	x	x	x	x	x	x	x			x					x	x	x	x	x	x	22
21						x	x		x	x	x				x	x				x	21
20			x	x			x	x	x	x					x	x				x	20
19		x	x			x	x			x	x				x	x				x	19
18		x	x			x	x			x		x	x		x	x				x	18
17	x	x				x	x		x	x	x				x	x			x	x	17
16	x			x	x		x	x	x	x	x				x	x			x	x	16
15			x	x			x	x		x		x	x		x	x				x	15
14			x	x			x	x		x		x	x		x	x				x	14
13	x	x			x	x				x			x	x		x	x			x	13
12	x			x	x					x			x	x		x	x		x	x	12
11	x	x			x	x				x			x	x		x	x			x	11
10		x	x			x	x			x		x	x		x	x				x	10
9			x	x			x	x		x		x	x		x	x				x	9
8	x			x	x		x	x	x	x	x				x	x			x	x	8
7	x	x				x	x		x	x	x				x	x			x	x	7
6		x	x			x	x			x		x	x		x	x				x	6
5			x	x			x	x		x		x	x		x	x				x	5
4				x	x		x	x	x	x	x				x	x				x	4
3				x	x		x	x	x						x	x				x	3
2	x	x	x	x	x	x	x			x			x	x	x	x	x	x	x	x	2
1																					1
Chart4	20	19	18	17	16	15	14	13	12	11	10	9	8	7	6	5	4	3	2	1	

» k 29 x 20 sts (complete pattern repeat) with BC and PC according to Chart 4.

» k 1 x the first 6 sts of Chart 4 with BC and PC according to Chart 4.

The sts on the left-hand side of the shawl (308 sts + 2 x (LFT + RT) inc 2 sts = 312 sts) are to be arranged as follows:

» k 1 x the last 6 sts of Chart 4 with BC and PC according to Chart 4.

» k 15 x 20 sts (complete pattern repeat) with BC and PC according to Chart 4.

» k 1 x the first 6 sts of Chart 4 with BC and PC according to Chart 4.

The sts on the left-hand side of the shawl (308 sts + 2 x (LFT + RT) inc 2 sts = 312 sts) are to be arranged as follows:

» k 1 x the last 6 sts of Chart 4 with BC and PC according to Chart 4.

» k 15 x 20 sts (complete pattern repeat) with BC and PC according to Chart 4.

» k 1 x the first 6 sts of Chart 4 with BC and PC according to Chart 4.

TIP: Place SM after each pattern repeat.

R 3-22: k the border pattern with BC and PC according to Chart 4.
Due to the continuous increases, the pattern must also be extended to the left and the right.

R 23: k with BC only.
R 24: p with the yarn colour according to Chart 4 (folding edge).
No increases are knitted at the three tips of the shawl.

Reverse side of the border

Now all increases previously made at the three tips of the shawl border front (2-st markers) must be decreased.

In each R before and after the 2-st-marker 1 st each has to be decreased left-leaning (ssk) and right-leaning (k2tog) accordingly.

This way 6 sts are being decreased in each round.

Please follow the pattern repeats as created for the front side of the border.

For the reverse side of the border knit rounds 23-1 of the border pattern.

Cast-off all sts and sew them to the inside of the border.
See the description of the "knit-and-sew cast-off" method (cf. pages 24-26)

Finishing the shawl

Wash and block the shawl. After drying the shawl, you might want to prepare tassels/pom-poms and sew them to the tips of the shawl together with felt balls.

ARABESQUE

In 2015, I visited the city of Marrakech. I was fascinated by the old town, the hustle and bustle of Djemaa el-Fna, the colours, the light, the architecture and the Arabic art of wood carvings. All this inspired me to create the pattern for the Arabesque shawl.

Yarn

Abbreviation	Yarn Manufacturer	Yardage/100g
G	Gardiner S08 Shetland (100% wool)	450m/100g
G1	Gardiner SS11 Soft Shetland (100% wool)	565m/100g
H	Harrisville New England Shetland (100% pure wool)	397m/100g
J	Jamieson of Shetland Shetland Spindrift (100% pure Shetland wool)	420m/100g
JU	Jamieson of Shetland Ultra (50% Shetland/50% lambswool)	776m/100g
K	Knoll Supersoft (100% PURE NEW WOOL)	576m/100g
SF	Lankava Esito worsted wool yarn (100% wool)	425m/100g
Ra	Rauma Finull PT2 (100% Norwegian wool)	350m/100g
Re	Rennie Supersoft (100% lambswool)	565m/100g
ReU	Rennie Unique Shetland (100% lambswool)	450m/100g
ReC	Rennie Supersoft Cashmere (87.5% lambswool/12.5% cashmere)	492m/100g
LT	Tines 100% wool	350m/100g

Shetland Spindrift, Supersoft (lambswool), pure new wool etc. The yardage of the different yarns varies. Further information can be found in the chapter concerning yarns and suppliers (see pp. 160-161).

Version 1 "Pine + Red-Coral-Pink Shades"

Yarn kit "Arabesque - Version 1" by Bärbel Salet VerstrickteKunst or

350 g pattern colour(s) (PC) Pine (J)

450 g background colour(s) (BC)
15 x 30 g #424 Red (Ra), Lelantos (ReC), Poppy (H), Scarlet (Re), Brandy (K), Zinnia (H), Coral (ReU), Salmon (Re), Geranium (K),
Sherbet (J), Fuchsia (J), Poppy (K), Plum (J), Pink (H), #4886 Dark Cherry (Ra)

The amount of yarn required for the border and the tassels/pom-poms is included in the above.

Version 2 "Port Wine + Powder Shades"

Yarn kit "Arabesque - Version 2" by Bärbel Salet VerstrickteKunst or

350 g pattern colour(s) (PC) Port Wine (J)

455 g background colour(s) (BC)
13 x 35 g Red Clover (K), Magenta Sky (ReC), Lipstick (J), #530 Raspberry (LT), Sorbet (J), Allium (K), #522 Flamingo (LT), Rose (J), Dog Rose (J), Blossom (J), Sugarsnap (K), Apricot (J), Peach (J)

The amount of yarn required for the border and the tassels/pom-poms is included in the above.

Chart1

Legend:

x	pattern colour(s)	A	chain cast-on stitch
(shaded)	background colour(s)	o	knit
I	cast-on stitches	+	purl bump increase
x (filled)	pattern starting point	RS	right side row
		WS	wrong side row

Chart columns are numbered 43 42 41 40 39 38 37 36 35 34 33 32 31 30 29 28 27 26 25 24 23 22 21 20 19 18 17 16 15 14 13 12 11 10 9 8 7 6 5 4 3 2 1 (read right to left).

Row	Side	Stitches
23	RS	(43 sts)
22	WS	(41 sts)
21	RS	(39 sts)
20	WS	(37 sts)
19	RS	(35 sts)
18	WS	(33 sts)
17	RS	(31 sts)
16	WS	(29 sts)
15	RS	(27 sts)
14	WS	(25 sts)
13	RS	(23 sts)
12	WS	(21 sts)
11	RS	(19 sts)
10	WS	(17 sts)
9	RS	(15 sts)
8	WS	(13 sts)
7	RS	(11 sts)
6	WS	(9 sts)
5	RS	(7 sts)
4	WS	(5 sts)
3	RS	(4 sts)
2	WS	
1	RS	

(Row 1 contains the 3 cast-on stitches [I I I]. Row 5 marks the pattern starting point [x]. Increase markers A, + and the knit marker o form the two converging diagonals at each edge; the x marks form the central Fair Isle motif.)

Arrangement of colours

The gradient colour schemes of both PC and BC are achieved with the help of previously prepared "magic balls", see the technical chapter, p. 13 ff. The wingspans are being determined individually.

Needles

3.25 mm circular needles (with different cable lengths); adjust needle size to obtain gauge if necessary.

DPNs might be useful at the beginning of the shawl.

3 sets of 3.25 mm circular needles with 100 cm cables for knitting the border; adjust needle size to obtain gauge if necessary.

Gauge

27 sts and 32 rows with 3.25 mm needles = 10 x 10 cm

Dimensions

Width 238 cm

Height 98 cm

Stitches

Stockinette stitch; two-colour Fair Isle knitting

Starting the shawl

R 1 cast-on row: co 3 sts with BC [I]

R 2 (WS): p 3 + chain cast-on 1 st [A]

R 3 (RS): k [o], k 3 sts = 4 sts, chain cast-on 1 st [A]

R 4 (WS): k [o], p 4 sts = 5 sts, chain cast-on 1 st [A]

R 5 (RS): This row marks the beginning/starting point of the patterned section.

From this row onwards 1 st is increased each at the beginning [A] and at the end [+].

K R 6 (WS) up to and including R 23 (RS).

Integration of steek stitches

R 23 (RS/43 sts on needle): At the end of this row chain cast-on 15 steek sts, alternating between BC and PC.
Close the row to a round.

Continue knitting either with DPNs or using the Magic Loop technique. From here onwards, only k stitches are being used.

Please change to Chart 2 / R 24.

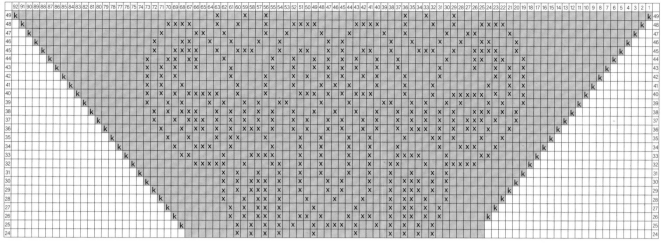

Chart2

x	pattern colour(s)	I	cast-on stitches	A	chain cast-on stitch	RS	right side row
	background colour(s)	x	pattern starting point	o	knit	WS	wrong side row
				+	purl bump increase	k	Kfb/knit front back

First round with steek stitches

Start knitting R 24 with the following partition (Chart 2):

» K 43 sts acc. to Chart 2.
» Place SM.
» K 14 steek sts according to the established colour scheme.
» Place SM.
» K the 15th steek st.

This first round with steek stitches does not feature any increase.

From R 25 up to and including R 49

» K all sts according to Chart 2/R 25.
» At the end of this R, inc 1 st by kfb from the last st.
» Move SM to the right needle.
» K 14 steek sts.
» Move SM to the right needle.
» Inc 1 st by kfb from the 15th steek stitch

At the end of R 49, there will be 92 sts on the needles (excluding the steek sts).

Mark the central 56 sts (19th up to and including 74th st) by placing SMs. On both sides of this central pattern repeat there will be 18 sts each.

Please change to Chart 3 / R 1.

All following rounds

» Inc 1 st by kfb from the 15th steek st.
» K the last 18 sts (39th st up to and including 56th st) acc. to Chart 3 / R 1.
» Move SM to the right needle.
» K the pattern repeats according to Chart 3 (56 sts).
» Move SM to the right needle.
» K the first 18 sts (1st st up to and including 18th st) acc. to Chart 3 / R 1. Inc 1 st by kfb from the last st of the row.
» Move SM to the right needle.
» K 14 steek sts.
» Move SM to the right needle.

As increases are regularly added, the pattern must also be extended to the right and left.

For better orientation, completed horizontal pattern repeats should be identified by the placement of SMs. Once the first pattern repeat has been achieved hight-wise, start again with R 1.

The pattern of Chart 3 is repeated 4 x vertically (4 x 57 rounds).

Finally, the 6 rounds of Chart 4 are to be knitted.

In the end the shawl will feature a total of 283 rounds.

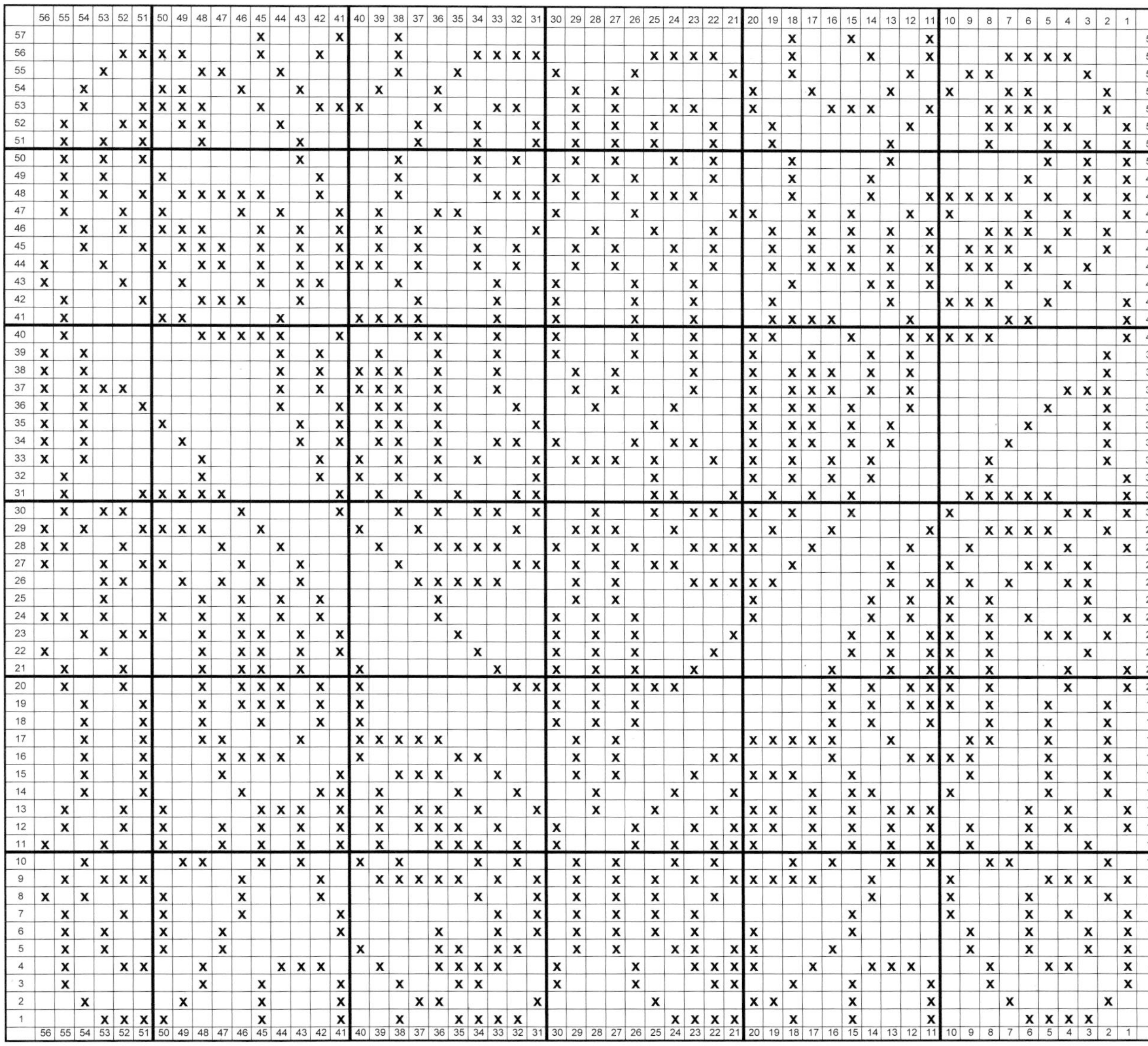

Chart 3

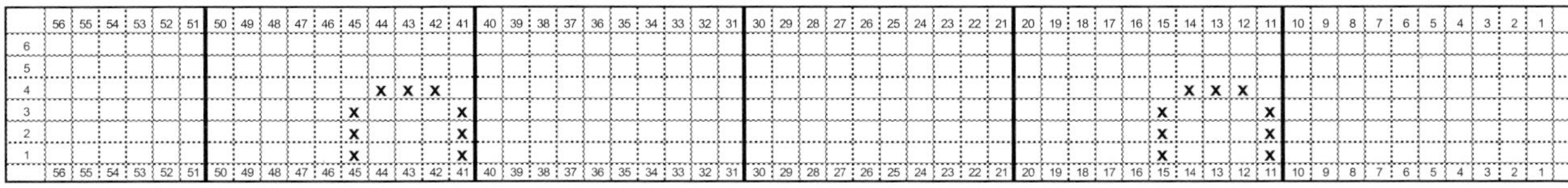

Chart 4

These can be split up as follows:
1 x 49 R (Chart 2)
4 x 57 R of the complete pattern repeat (Chart 3) = 288 R
6 R (1st to 6th rows of the pattern repeat as per Chart 4)

The pattern is repeated 9 times horizontally in total (9 x 56 sts = 504 sts) plus the last 28 sts of a pattern repeat on the upper right tip and the first 28 sts of a pattern repeat on the upper right tip = 560 sts.

Chart 5

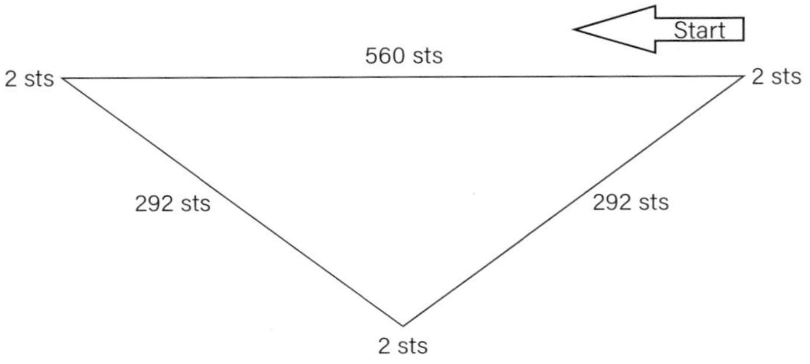

Triangle diagram:
- Top edge: 560 sts
- Left side: 292 sts
- Right side: 292 sts
- Top-left: 2 sts
- Top-right: 2 sts
- Bottom tip: 2 sts
- Start (arrow pointing left at top right)

Version 1
BC = red-coral-pink shades "magic ball"
PC = Pine (J)

Version 2
BC = powder shades "magic ball"
PC = Port Wine (J)

Chart 6

	12	11	10	9	8	7	6	5	4	3	2	1	
16				FOLDING EDGE [PURL]									16
15	x	x	x	x	x	x	x	x	x	x	x	x	15
14	x		x	x	x		x	x	x		x	x	14
13				x			x					x	13
12	x		x			x		x			x	x	12
11	x	x			x	x	x			x	x	x	11
10	x			x	x		x	x			x	x	10
9			x	x			x	x				x	9
8		x	x			x			x	x			8
7			x	x				x	x			x	7
6	x			x	x		x	x			x	x	6
5	x	x			x	x	x			x	x	x	5
4	x		x			x			x		x	x	4
3				x			x					x	3
2	x		x	x	x		x	x	x		x	x	2
1	x	x	x	x	x	x	x	x	x	x	x	x	1
	12	11	10	9	8	7	6	5	4	3	2	1	

Cutting the steek

Bind off steek sts 2 until 14 inclusive. Moisten and block the steek. When dry, secure the steek and cut it open.

Border

K all 560 sts of the upper edge with Pine (J) for Version 1 or Port Wine (J) for Version 2.
Inc 1 st by kfb from the 1st steek st and place SM (left tip; 2-st-marker).
Pick up and knit 292 sts on the left side.
At the bottom tip inc 2 sts and place SM (2-st-marker).
Pick up and knit 292 sts on the right side.
Inc 1 st by kfb from the 15th steek st and place SM (right tip; 2-st-marker).

BORDER PATTERN

At each of the 2-st-markers inc 1 st on both sides by M1R and M1L.
The sts of the 2-st-markers are always knitted with BC.
Each round will thus feature an increase of 6 sts.

R 1: k with BC.
Arrange the 24 sts of the pattern repeat evenly and mark the single repeats with SMs.
Please be reminded to regularly increase (2-st-markers) at all three tips of the shawl. Due to the continuous increases, the pattern must also be extended to the left and the right.

R 2-14: k the border pattern with BC and PC according to Chart 5.
R 15: k with PC only.
R 16: p with the PC only (folding edge). No increases are knitted at the three tips of the shawl.

Reverse side of the border

Now all increases previously made at the three tips of the shawl border front (2-st markers) must be decreased.
In each R before and after the 2-st-marker 1 st each has to be decreased left-leaning (ssk) and right-leaning (k2tog) accordingly.
This way 6 sts are being decreased in each round.
Please follow the pattern repeats as created for the front side of the border.
Cast-off all sts and sew them to the inside of the border.
See the description of the "knit-and-sew cast-off" method (see pp. 24-26)

Finishing the shawl

Wash and block the shawl.
After drying the shawl, you might want to prepare tassels/pom-poms and sew them to the tips of the shawl together with felt balls.

TRACERY

It took me a while to find the right name for this shawl.
Maria-Theresia from Salzburg said that the pattern reminded her of
church windows and the English term of "Tracery" would fit
perfectly. The term itself probably derives from the tracing floors on
which the complex patterns of windows were laid out in late Gothic
architecture.

Yarn

Abbreviation	Yarn Manufacturer	Yardage/100g
G	Gardiner S08 Shetland (100% wool)	450m/100g
G1	Gardiner SS11 Soft Shetland (100% wool)	565m/100g
H	Harrisville New England Shetland (100% pure wool)	397m/100g
J	Jamieson of Shetland Shetland Spindrift (100% pure Shetland wool)	420m/100g
JU	Jamieson of Shetland Ultra (50% Shetland/50% lambswool)	776m/100g
K	Knoll Supersoft (100% PURE NEW WOOL)	576m/100g
SF	Lankava Esito worsted wool yarn (100% wool)	425m/100g
Ra	Rauma Finull PT2 (100% Norwegian wool)	350m/100g
Re	Rennie Supersoft (100% lambswool)	565m/100g
ReU	Rennie Unique Shetland (100% lambswool)	450m/100g
ReC	Rennie Supersoft Cashmere (87.5% lambswool/12.5% cashmere)	492m/100g
LT	Tines 100% wool	350m/100g

Shetland Spindrift, Supersoft (lambswool), pure new wool etc. The yardage of the different yarns varies. Further information can be found in the chapter concerning yarns and suppliers (see pp. 160-161).

Version 1 "Purple + Berry Shades"

Yarn kit "Tracery - Version 1" by Bärbel Salet VerstrickteKunst or

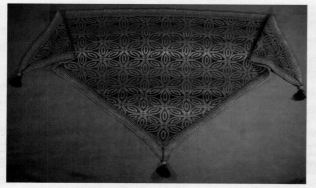

390 g pattern colour(s) (PC)

13 x 30 g Mantilla (J), Plum (K), Petunia (Re), Magenta (H), Amaranth Mix (Re), Elderberry (G), Raspberry (H), Carnation (Re), Pink (H), Plum (J), Lavish (Re), Chianti (H), Cherry (J)

420 g background colour(s) (BC)

7 x 60 g Mulberry (J), Blackberry (H), Black Cherry (H), Zodiac (J), Blueberry (Re), Purple Haze (K), Prussian (K)

The amount of yarn required for the border and the tassels/pompoms is included in the above.

Version 2 "Green + Elderberry

Yarn kit "Tracery - Version 2" by Bärbel Salet VerstrickteKunst or

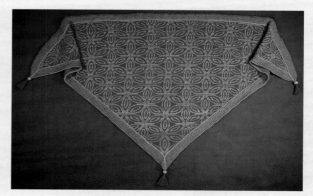

440 g pattern colour(s) (PC)

2 x 70 g New Lawn (Re), Kiwi (H),

4 x 75 g Grass (G), #345 Jungle (LT), Garden Leaf (Re), #458 Grün (Ra)

370 g Hintergrundfarbe(n) (HG)

Elderberry (G)

The amount of yarn required for the border and the tassels/pompoms is included in the above.

Chart 1

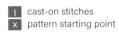
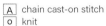

Row		sts		43	42	41	40	39	38	37	36	35	34	33	32	31	30	29	28	27	26	25	24	23	22	21	20	19	18	17	16	15	14	13	12	11	10	9	8	7	6	5	4	3	2	1		sts		Row
23		(43 sts)	+		x	x	x	x	x	x							x	x				x	x				x	x				x	x					x	x	x	x	x		o				RS	23
22	WS			o			x	x	x	x						x	x				x	x				x	x				x	x				x	x	x	x				+	A	(41 sts)		22
21		(39 sts)	A	+			x	x	x						x	x				x	x				x	x				x	x				x	x	x						o				RS	21
20	WS				o			x	x	x					x	x				x	x			x	x	x				x	x				x	x	x					+	A		(37 sts)		20
19		(35 sts)		A	+			x	x	x				x	x				x	x				x	x				x	x			x	x	x					o					RS	19
18	WS					o			x	x				x	x				x	x		x	x	x	x	x				x	x				x	x					+	A		(33 sts)		18
17		(31 sts)			A	+			x	x				x	x				x	x			x	x	x				x	x			x	x				o						RS	17
16	WS						o			x	x			x	x			x	x				x				x	x		x	x							+	A			(29 sts)		16
15		(27 sts)				A	+			x	x			x	x			x	x				x	x			x	x		x	x				o								RS	15
14	WS							o			x	x		x	x		x	x			x	x			x	x		x	x						+	A				(25 sts)		14
13		(23 sts)					A	+		x	x		x	x	x	x		x	x		x	x	x	x		x	x		x	x			o								RS	13
12	WS								o		x	x		x	x		x	x			x	x		x	x			+	A					(21 sts)		12
11		(19 sts)						A	+		x	x	x	x	x	x	x	x	x	x	x	x			o										RS	11
10	WS								o		x	x		x	x		x	x		x	x		+	A					(17 sts)		10
9		(15 sts)							A	+		x	x		x	x		x	x		o					RS	9
8	WS									o	x	x	x	x		x	x	x	x		+	A				(13 sts)		8
7		(11 sts)								A	+	x	x		x		x		x	x	o					RS	7
6	WS										o	x	x	x	x	x	x	+	A			(9 sts)		6
5		(7 sts)									A	+			x			o					RS	5
4	WS											o				A				(5 sts)		4
3		(4 sts)										A		o					RS	3
2	WS											A					2
1																			I	I	I						RS	1

Legend:

x	pattern colour(s)	I	cast-on stitches	A	chain cast-on stitch	RS	right side row
(grey)	background colour(s)	x	pattern starting point	o	knit	WS	wrong side row
				+	purl bump increase		

Arrangement of colours

The gradient colour schemes of both PC and BC are achieved with the help of previously prepared "magic balls", see the technical chapter, p. 13 ff. The wingspans are being determined individually.

Needles

3.25 mm circular needles (with different cable lengths); adjust needle size to obtain gauge if necessary.
DPNs might be useful at the beginning of the shawl.
3 sets of 3.25 mm circular needles with 100 cm cables for knitting the border.

Gauge

27 sts and 32 rows with 3.25 mm needles = 10 x 10 cm

Dimensions

Width 239 cm
Height 107 cm

Stitches

Stockinette stitch; two-colour Fair Isle knitting

Starting the shawl

R 1 cast-on row: co 3 sts with BC [|]
R 2 (WS): p 3 + chain cast-on 1 st [A]
R 3 (RS): k [o], k 3 sts = 4 sts, chain cast-on 1 st [A]
R 4 (WS): k [o], p 4 sts = 5 sts, chain cast-on 1 st [A]
R 5 (RS): This row marks the beginning/starting point of the patterned section.
From this row onwards, 1 st is increased each at the beginning [A] and at the end [+].
K R 6 (WS) up to and including R 23 (RS).

Integration of steek stitches

R 23 (RS/43 sts on needle): At the end of this row chain cast-on 15 steek sts, alternating between BC and PC. Close the row to a round. From now on all sts are k sts. Continue knitting either with DPNs or using the Magic Loop technique.

Please change to Chart 2 / R 24.

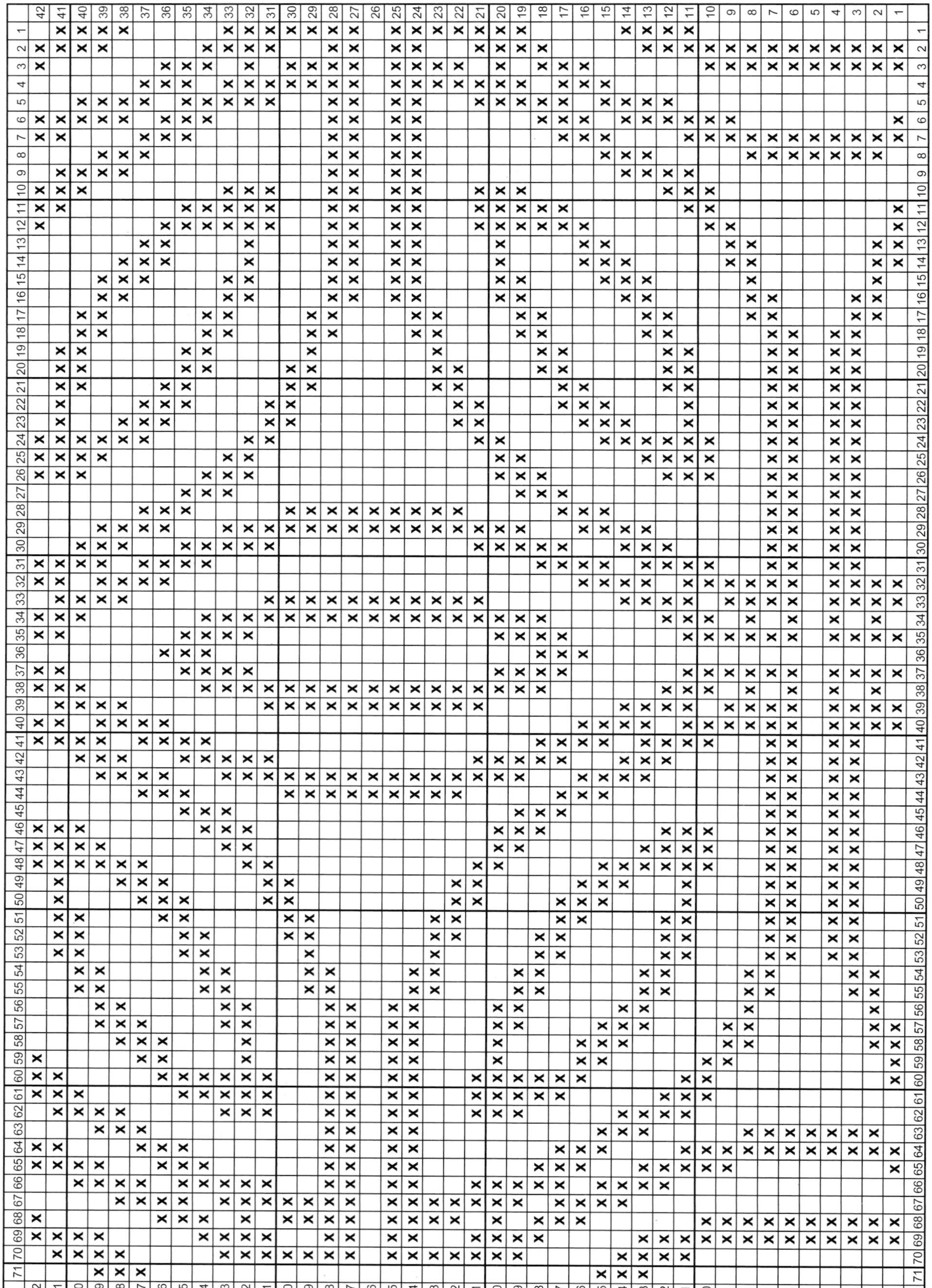

Chart 2

Chart3

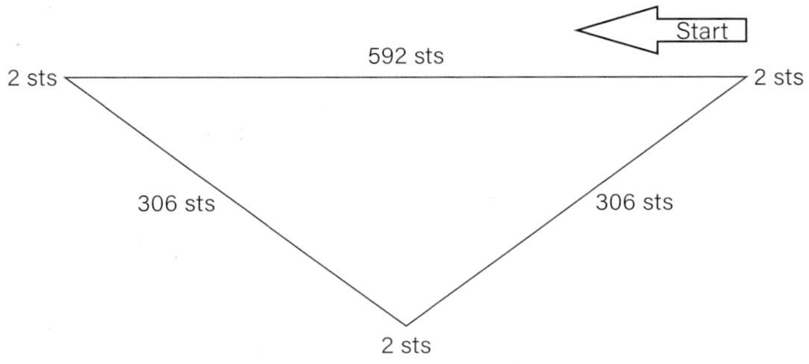

Start

592 sts

2 sts   2 sts

306 sts   306 sts

2 sts

First round with steek stitches

Start knitting R 24 with the following partition (Chart 2):

» K from st 15 up to and including st 57.
» Place SM.
» K 14 steek sts according to the established colour scheme.
» Place SM.
» K the 15th steek st.

This first round with steek stitches does not feature any increase.

From R 25 onwards and all following rounds

» K all sts according to Chart 2/R 25.
» At the end of this R, inc 1 st by kfb from the last st.
» Move SM to the right needle.
» K 14 steek sts.
» Move SM to the right needle.
» Inc 1 st by kfb from the 15th steek stitch

As increases are regularly added, the pattern must also be extended to the right and left.

For better orientation, completed horizontal pattern repeats should be identified by the placement of SMs. Once the first pattern repeat has been achieved hight-wise, start again with R 1.

In the end the shawl will be 299 rounds high (7 x 42 R of the complete pattern repeat plus one partial repeat from R 1 to and including R 4 + 1 R k with BC) and 592 sts wide.

The pattern is repeated 7 times horizontally in total (7 x 71 sts = 497 sts) plus the first 47 sts of a pattern repeat plus 1 st from the 299th round on the upper left tip = 48 sts and the last 46 sts of a pattern repeat plus 1 st from the 299th round = 47 sts on the upper right tip.
= 592 Maschen

Cutting the steek

Bind off steek sts 2 until 14 inclusive. Moisten and block the steek. When dry, secure the steek and cut it open.

Version 1
BC = purple "magic ball "
PC = "magic ball" in berry shades

Version 2
BC = green "magic ball"
PC = Elderberry (G)

Border

K all 592 sts of the upper edge with the "magic ball" in berry shades (PC) for Version 1 or with the green "magic ball" (BC) for Version 2.

Inc 1 st by kfb from the 1st steek st and place SM (left tip; 2-st-marker).
Pick up and knit 306 sts on the left side.
At the bottom tip inc 2 sts and place SM (2-st-marker).
Pick up and knit 306 sts on the right side.

Inc 1 st by kfb from the 15th steek st and place SM (right tip; 2-st-marker).

Purl one round with the "magic ball" in berry shades (PC) for Version 1 or with the green "magic ball" (BC) for Version 2 (eyecatcher line).

At each of the 2-st-markers inc 1 st on both sides by M1R and M1L.

Each round will thus feature an increase of 6 sts.

	18	17	16	15	14	13	12	11	10	9	8	7	6	5	4	3	2	1	
21			F	O	L	D	I	N	G	E	D	G	E	[	P	U	R	L]	21
20	x	x	x	x	x	x	x	x	x	x	x	x	x	x	x	x	x	x	20
19																			19
18	x	x	x	x	x	x	x	x	x	x	x	x	x	x	x	x		x	18
17															x			x	17
16		x	x	x	x	x	x	x	x	x	x	x	x	x	x			x	16
15		x													x			x	15
14		x	x	x	x	x	x	x	x	x	x	x			x			x	14
13		x		x							x				x			x	13
12		x		x	x	x	x	x	x			x			x			x	12
11		x		x					x		x				x			x	11
10		x		x		x	x	x	x		x				x			x	10
9		x		x		x			x		x				x			x	9
8		x		x		x		x	x	x	x				x			x	8
7		x		x		x					x				x			x	7
6		x		x		x	x	x	x	x	x				x			x	6
5		x		x											x			x	5
4		x		x	x	x	x	x	x	x	x	x	x	x				x	4
3		x																x	3
2		x	x	x	x	x	x	x	x	x	x	x	x	x	x	x	x	x	2
1																			1
	18	17	16	15	14	13	12	11	10	9	8	7	6	5	4	3	2	1	

Chart 4

BORDER PATTERN

R 1: k with BC.
The sts of the 2-st-markers are always knitted with BC.

Arrange the 18 sts of the pattern repeat evenly and mark the single repeats with SMs.

Please be reminded to regularly increase (2-st-markers) at all three tips of the shawl. Due to the continuous increases, the pattern must also be extended to the left and the right.

R 2-18: k the border pattern with BC and PC.
R 19: k with BC only.
R 20: k with PC for Version 1 or with BC for Version 2.
R 18: p with PC for Version 1 or with BC for Version 2 (folding edge). No increases are knitted at the three tips of the shawl.

Reverse side of the border

In each R before and after the 2-st-marker 1 st each has to be decreased left-leaning (ssk) and right-leaning (k2tog) accordingly.

This way 6 sts are being decreased in each round.

Please follow the pattern repeats as created for the front side of the border.

For the reverse side of the border, please k rows 20 to 1 of the border pattern.

Cast-off all sts and sew them to the inside of the border. See the description of the "knit-and-sew cast-off" method (see pp. 24-26).

Finishing the shawl

Wash and block the shawl.
After drying the shawl, you might want to prepare tassels/pom-poms and sew them to the tips of the shawl together with felt balls.

VINEYARD

I got the inspiration for this design during one of my workshops. The colour scheme was developed with one of the participants for this shawl. The result was so beautiful that I had to incorporate this colour scheme into a pattern I designed myself. The colours remind me of a vineyard covered in autumn foliage.

Yarn

Abbreviation	Yarn Manufacturer	Yardage/100g
G	Gardiner S08 Shetland (100% wool)	450m/100g
G1	Gardiner SS11 Soft Shetland (100% wool)	565m/100g
H	Harrisville New England Shetland (100% pure wool)	397m/100g
J	Jamieson of Shetland Shetland Spindrift (100% pure Shetland wool)	420m/100g
JU	Jamieson of Shetland Ultra (50% Shetland/50% lambswool)	776m/100g
K	Knoll Supersoft (100% PURE NEW WOOL)	576m/100g
SF	Lankava Esito worsted wool yarn (100% wool)	425m/100g
Ra	Rauma Finull PT2 (100% Norwegian wool)	350m/100g
Re	Rennie Supersoft (100% lambswool)	565m/100g
ReU	Rennie Unique Shetland (100% lambswool)	450m/100g
ReC	Rennie Supersoft Cashmere (87.5% lambswool/12.5% cashmere)	492m/100g
LT	Tines 100% wool	350m/100g

Shetland Spindrift, Supersoft (lambswool), pure new wool etc. The yardage of the different yarns varies. Further information can be found in the chapter concerning yarns and suppliers (see pp. 160-161).

Version 1 "Petrol + Autumn Shades"

Yarn kit "Vineyard - Version 1" by Bärbel Salet VerstrickteKunst or

306 g pattern colour(s) (PC)

18 x 17 g Madder (J), Ginger (J), Saffron (K), Iron Rust (Re), Ember (K), #8026 Orange-brown (SF), Hephaestus (ReC), #740 Orange (LT), Pumpkin (J), Jaffa (Re), Spice (Re), Paprika (J), Russet (H), Garnet (H), #497 Burgundy (Ra), Port Wine (J), Bordeaux Mix (Re), Maroon (J)

280 g background colour(s) (BC)

5 x 56 g Loden Blue (H), Storm (Re), Petrel (Re), Petrel (G), Vintage Heather (K)

110 g Calypso (Re) for border (PC) and tassels/pom-poms
110 g Petrel (Re) for border (BC) and tassels/pom-poms

The amount of yarn required for the border and the tassels/pom-poms is included in the above.

Version 2 " Green-Yellow-Green + Fuchsia + Coral + Grenadine"

Yarn kit "Vineyard - Version 2" by Bärbel Salet VerstrickteKunst or

308 g pattern colour(s) (PC)

11 x 28 g Poppy (K), Grenadine (Re), Poppy (J), Zinnia (H), Coral (ReU), Salmon (Re), Flame (J), Perfect Peach (Re), Geranium (K), Sherbet (J), Fuchsia (J)

280 g background colour(s) (BC)

8 x 35 g Grass (H), Tundra (H), #8034 Lime green (SF), Calypso (K), Stonehenge (Re), Spring Meadow (Re), #8040 Leaf green (SF), Calypso (Re)

110 g Cherry (J) for border (PC) and tassels/pom-poms
110 g Calypso (Re) for border (BC)

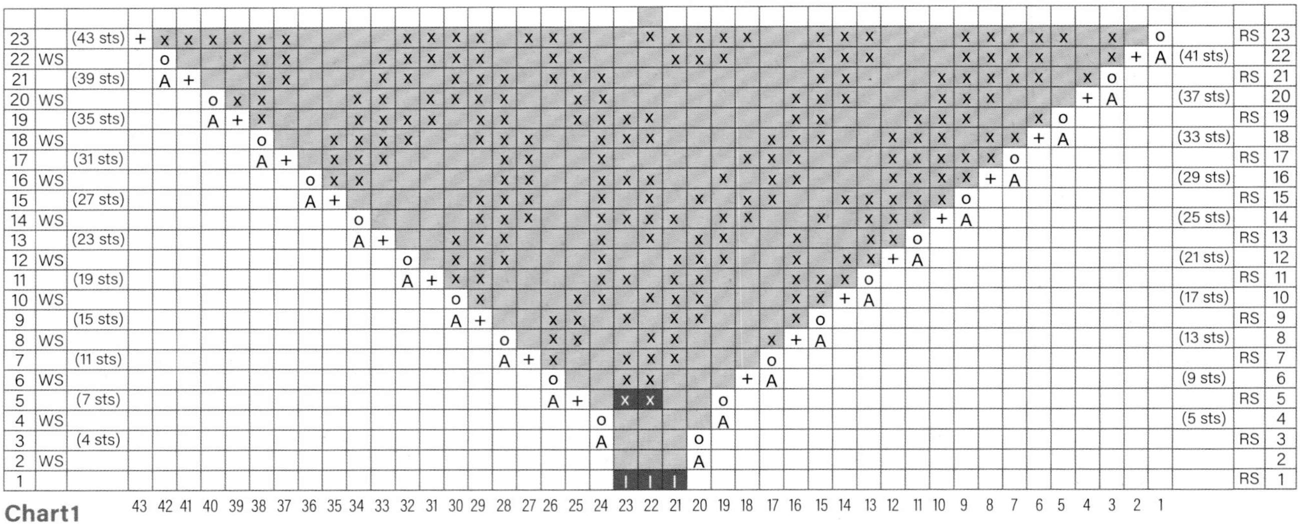

Chart1

Column numbers (left to right): 43 42 41 40 39 38 37 36 35 34 33 32 31 30 29 28 27 26 25 24 23 22 21 20 19 18 17 16 15 14 13 12 11 10 9 8 7 6 5 4 3 2 1

Row	Side	sts (start)	sts (end)	Side	Row
23		(43 sts)		RS	23
22	WS		(41 sts)		22
21		(39 sts)		RS	21
20	WS		(37 sts)		20
19		(35 sts)		RS	19
18	WS		(33 sts)		18
17		(31 sts)		RS	17
16	WS		(29 sts)		16
15		(27 sts)		RS	15
14	WS		(25 sts)		14
13		(23 sts)		RS	13
12	WS		(21 sts)		12
11		(19 sts)		RS	11
10	WS		(17 sts)		10
9		(15 sts)		RS	9
8	WS		(13 sts)		8
7		(11 sts)		RS	7
6	WS		(9 sts)		6
5		(7 sts)		RS	5
4	WS		(5 sts)		4
3		(4 sts)		RS	3
2	WS				2
1				RS	1

Legend:

x	pattern colour(s)
(grey)	background colour(s)
I	cast-on stitches
x (highlighted)	pattern starting point
A	chain cast-on stitch
o	knit
+	purl bump increase
RS	right side row
WS	wrong side row

Arrangement of colours

Version 1

The gradient colour scheme of both PC was achieved with the help of previously prepared "magic ball", see the technical chapter, p. 13 ff. For the background colour scheme, it is not necessary to prepare a "magic ball". Here BC is being "adjusted" to fit PC, i.e., the dark PCs such as Bordeaux Mix, Port Wine etc. were combined with BC Loden Blue or Storm. These are slightly lighter if compared to Vintage Heather and the two shades of petrol. Contrast is the keyword!

Version 2

The gradient colour schemes of both PC and BC are achieved with the help of previously prepared "magic balls", see the technical chapter, p. 13 ff. The wingspans are being determined individually. Artistic licence!

Needles

3.25 mm circular needles (with different cable lengths); adjust needle size to obtain gauge if necessary.
DPNs might be useful at the beginning of the shawl.
3 sets of 3.25 mm circular needles with 100 cm cables for knitting the border; adjust needle size to obtain gauge if necessary.

Gauge

27 sts and 32 rows with 3.25 mm needles = 10 x 10 cm

Dimensions

Width 241 cm
Height 106 cm

Stitches

Stockinette stitch; two-colour Fair Isle knitting

Starting the shawl

R 1 cast-on row: co 3 sts with BC [|]
R 2 (WS): p 3 + chain cast-on 1 st [A]
R 3 (RS): k [o], k 3 sts = 4 sts, chain cast-on 1 st [A]
R 4 (WS): k [o], p 4 sts = 5 sts, chain cast-on 1 st [A]
R 5 (RS): This row marks the beginning/starting point of the patterned section. From this row onwards 1 st is increased each at the beginning [A] and at the end [+].

K R 6 (WS) up to and including R 23 (RS).

Integration of steek stitches

R 23 (RS/43 sts on needle): At the end of this row chain cast-on 15 steek sts, alternating between BC and PC. Close the row to a round. From now on all sts are k sts. Continue knitting either with DPNs or using the Magic Loop technique

Please change to Chart 2 / R 24.

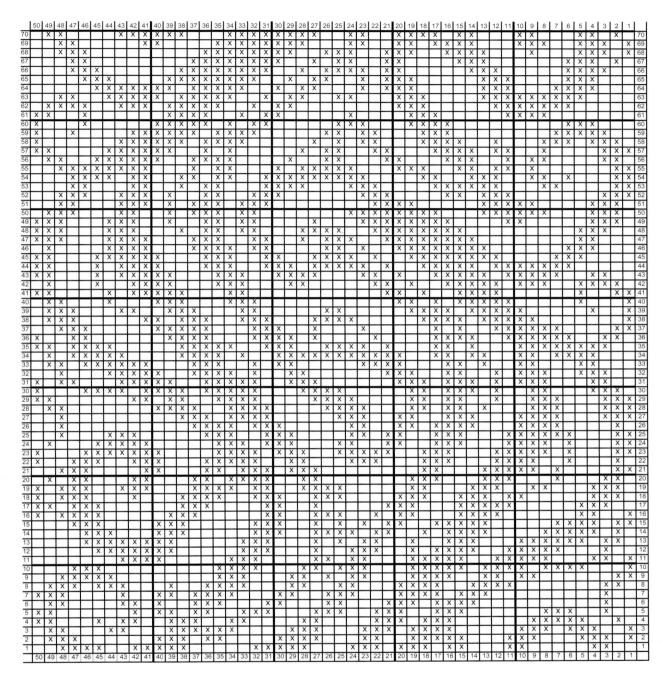

First round with steek stitches

Start knitting R 24 with the following partition (Chart 2):

» K from st 4 up to and including st 46.

» Place SM.

» K 14 steek sts according to the established colour scheme.

» Place SM.

» K the 15th steek st.

This first round with steek stitches does not feature any increase.

Chart 2

From R 25 onwards and all following rounds

- » K all sts according to Chart 2/R 25.
- » At the end of this R, inc 1 st by kfb from the last st.
- » Move SM to the right needle.
- » K 14 steek sts.
- » Move SM to the right needle.
- » Inc 1 st by kfb from the 15th steek stitch.

As increases are regularly added, the pattern must also be extended to the right and left. For better orientation, completed horizontal pattern repeats should be identified by the placement of SMs. Once the first pattern repeat has been achieved hight-wise, start again with R 1.

In the end the shawl will be 306 rounds high (4 x 70 R of the complete pattern repeat plus one partial repeat from R 1 to and including R 26) and 606 sts wide.

The pattern is repeated 11 times horizontally in total (11 x 50 sts = 550 sts) plus the first 28 sts of a pattern repeat on the upper left tip and the last 28 sts of a pattern repeat on the upper right tip.
= 606 sts

Cutting the steek

Bind off steek sts 2 until 14 inclusive. Moisten and block the steek. When dry, secure the steek and cut it open.

Border

K all 606 sts of the upper edge with Calypso (Re) for Version 1 or Cherry (J) for Version 2.

Inc 1 st by kfb from the 1st steek st and place SM (left tip; 2-st-marker).
Pick up and knit 300 sts on the left side.
At the bottom tip inc 2 sts and place SM (2-st-marker).

Pick up and knit 300 sts on the right side.
Inc 1 st by kfb from the 15th steek st and place SM (right tip; 2-st-marker).
Purl one rd with Calypso (Re) for Version 1 or Cherry (J) for Version 2 (eyecatcher line).

At each of the 2-st-markers inc 1 st on both sides by M1R and M1L.

Each round will thus feature an increase of 6 sts.

Chart 3

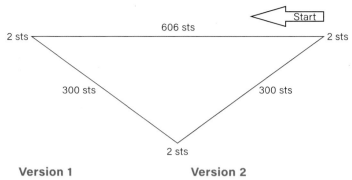

Version 1
BC = Vintage Heather (K)
PC = Calypso (Re)

Version 2
BC = Calypso (Re)
PC = Cherry (J)

BORDER PATTERN

	12	11	10	9	8	7	6	5	4	3	2	1	
19	F	O	L	D	I	N	G		E	D	G	E	19
18	x	x	x	x	x	x	x	x	x	x	x	x	18
17													17
16		x	x	x					x	x	x		16
15	x				x		x				x		15
14	x				x		x				x		14
13	x				x		x				x		13
12		x	x	x				x	x	x			12
11	x				x	x	x			x	x		11
10		x		x			x		x				10
9		x		x			x		x				9
8		x		x			x		x				8
7	x				x	x	x			x	x		7
6		x	x	x				x	x	x			6
5	x				x		x				x		5
4	x				x		x				x		4
3	x				x		x				x		3
2		x	x	x				x	x	x			2
1													1
	12	11	10	9	8	7	6	5	4	3	2	1	

Chart4

R 1: k with BC.

The sts of the 2-st-markers are always knitted with BC.

Arrange the 18 sts of the pattern repeat evenly and mark the single repeats with SMs.

Please be reminded to regularly increase (2-st-markers) at all three tips of the shawl.

R 2-16: k the border pattern with BC and PC according to Chart 4.
R 17: k with BC only.
R 18: k with PC only.
R 19: p with PC (folding edge). No increases are knitted at the three tips of the shawl.

Reverse side of the border

Now all increases previously made at the three tips of the shawl border front (2-st markers) must be decreased.

In each R before and after the 2-st-marker 1 st each has to be decreased left-leaning (ssk) and right-leaning (k2tog) accordingly.

This way 6 sts are being decreased in each round.

Please follow the pattern repeats as created for the front side of the border.

For the reverse side of the border please knit R 18-1 of the border pattern.

Cast-off all sts and sew them to the inside of the border. See the description of the "knit-and-sew cast-off" method (cf. pages 24-26).

Finishing the shawl

Wash and block the shawl. After drying the shawl, you might want to prepare tassels/pom-poms and sew them to the tips of the shawl together with felt balls.

EASYGOING

The inspiration for this shawl's colour scheme I got during a trip to England. I visited one of the many parks in Kent, where I discovered a weather-beaten turquoise door set into a brick wall.

Yarn

Abbreviation	Yarn Manufacturer	Yardage/100g
G	Gardiner S08 Shetland (100% wool)	450m/100g
G1	Gardiner SS11 Soft Shetland (100% wool)	565m/100g
H	Harrisville New England Shetland (100% pure wool)	397m/100g
J	Jamieson of Shetland Shetland Spindrift (100% pure Shetland wool)	420m/100g
JU	Jamieson of Shetland Ultra (50% Shetland/50% lambswool)	776m/100g
K	Knoll Supersoft (100% PURE NEW WOOL)	576m/100g
SF	Lankava Esito worsted wool yarn (100% wool)	425m/100g
Ra	Rauma Finull PT2 (100% Norwegian wool)	350m/100g
Re	Rennie Supersoft (100% lambswool)	565m/100g
ReU	Rennie Unique Shetland (100% lambswool)	450m/100g
ReC	Rennie Supersoft Cashmere (87.5% lambswool/12.5% cashmere)	492m/100g
LT	Tines 100% wool	350m/100g

Shetland Spindrift, Supersoft (lambswool), pure new wool etc. The yardage of the different yarns varies. Further information can be found in the chapter concerning yarns and suppliers (see pp. 160-161).

Version 1 "Turquoise + Orange-Red-Terracotta"

Yarn kit "Easygoing - Version 1" by Bärbel Salet VerstrickteKunst or

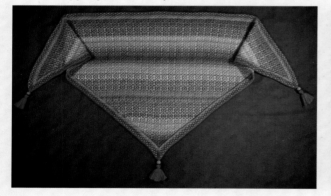

360 g pattern colour(s) (PC)

9 x 40 g #435 Cyan (LT), Aquamarine (K), Marble Gemstone (Re), Caspian (J), Mineral Blue (G), Aegean (H), Neptune (G1), Azure (Re), Larkspur (K)

420 g background colour(s) (BC)

12 x 35 g Henna (ReU), Paprika (J), Topaz (H), Ember (K), Amber (J), Hephaestus (ReC), Burnt Orange (K), Jaffa (Re), Spice (Re), Iron Rust (Re), Saffron (K), Ginger (J)

The amount of yarn required for the border and the tassels/pompoms is included in the above.

Version 2 "Orange + Natural Whites"

Yarn kit "Easygoing - Version 2" by Bärbel Salet VerstrickteKunst or

360 g pattern colour(s) (PC)

6 x 50 g #8025 Orange (SF), Pumpkin (J), Hephaestus (ReC), Clementine (K), Jaffa (Re), Spice (Re)
1 x 60 g Melon (H)

425 g background colour(s) (BC)

5 x 85 g Sand (G), Bleached White (K), Almond (K), Sand (J), Eesit (J)

The amount of yarn required for the border and the tassels/pompoms is included in the above.

Chart 1

Row													Side	Row
23	(43 sts)												RS	23
22	WS										(41 sts)			22
21	(39 sts)												RS	21
20	WS										(37 sts)			20
19	(35 sts)												RS	19
18	WS										(33 sts)			18
17	(31 sts)												RS	17
16	WS										(29 sts)			16
15	(27 sts)												RS	15
14	WS										(25 sts)			14
13	(23 sts)												RS	13
12	WS										(21 sts)			12
11	(19 sts)												RS	11
10	WS										(17 sts)			10
9	(15 sts)												RS	9
8	WS										(13 sts)			8
7	(11 sts)												RS	7
6	WS										(9 sts)			6
5	(7 sts)												RS	5
4	WS										(5 sts)			4
3	(4 sts)												RS	3
2	WS													2
1													RS	1

Legend:

- **x** pattern colour(s)
- (grey) background colour(s)
- **|** cast-on stitches
- **x** (dark) pattern starting point
- **A** chain cast-on stitch
- **o** knit
- **+** purl bump increase
- RS right side row
- WS wrong side row

Arrangement of colours

Version 1

The gradient colour schemes of both PC and BC are achieved with the help of previously prepared "magic balls", see the technical chapter, p. 13 ff. The wingspans are being determined individually.

Version 2

The gradient colour schemes of both PC and BC are achieved with the help of previously prepared "magic balls", see the technical chapter, p. 13 ff. The colour gradient for BC is wound from Eesit (J) to Sand (G) and back again. This way there are no hard colour transitions at all.

Needles

3.25 mm circular needles (with different cable lengths); adjust needle size to obtain gauge if necessary.
DPNs might be useful at the beginning of the shawl.
3 sets of 3.25 mm circular needles with 100 cm cables for knitting the border; adjust needle size to obtain gauge if necessary.

Gauge

27 sts and 32 rows with 3.25 mm needles = 10 x 10 cm

Dimensions

Width 240 cm
Height 105 cm

Stitches

Stockinette stitch; two-colour Fair Isle knitting

Starting the shawl

R 1 cast-on row: co 3 sts with BC [|]
R 2 (WS): p 3 + chain cast-on 1 st [A]
R 3 (RS): k [o], k 3 sts = 4 sts, chain cast-on 1 st [A]
R 4 (WS): k [o], p 4 sts = 5 sts, chain cast-on 1 st [A]
R 5 (RS): This row marks the beginning/starting point of the patterned section. From this row onwards 1 st is increased each at the beginning [A] and at the end [+].

K R 6 (WS) up to and including R 23 (RS) acc. to Chart 1.

TIP: In row 15, new repeats begin on both the left and right side of the central repeat. Mark these with SMs.

Integration of steek stitches

R 23 (RS/43 sts on needle): At the end of this row chain cast-on 15 steek sts, alternating between BC and PC. Close the row to a round. From now on all sts are k sts. Continue knitting either with DPNs or using the Magic Loop technique

Please change to Chart 2 / R 24.

	24	23	22	21	20	19	18	17	16	15	14	13	12	11	10	9	8	7	6	5	4	3	2	1	
24	X	X		X			X			X		X	X	X		X			X			X		X	24
23	X				X				X				X				X				X				23
22	X	X		X	X	X		X	X	X		X	X	X		X	X	X		X	X	X		X	22
21	X				X				X				X				X				X				21
20	X	X		X			X			X		X	X	X		X			X			X		X	20
19	X	X	X			X	X	X			X	X	X	X	X			X	X	X			X	X	19
18	X	X			X	X		X	X			X	X	X			X	X		X	X			X	18
17	X			X	X				X	X			X			X	X				X	X			17
16			X	X			X			X	X				X	X			X			X	X		16
15	X			X	X				X	X			X			X	X				X	X			15
14	X	X			X	X		X	X			X	X	X			X	X		X	X			X	14
13	X	X	X			X	X	X			X	X	X	X	X			X	X	X			X	X	13
12	X	X		X			X			X		X	X	X		X			X			X		X	12
11	X				X				X				X				X				X				11
10	X	X		X	X	X		X	X	X		X	X	X		X	X	X		X	X	X		X	10
9	X				X				X				X				X				X				9
8	X	X		X			X			X		X	X	X		X			X			X		X	8
7	X	X	X			X	X	X			X	X	X	X	X			X	X	X			X	X	7
6	X	X			X	X		X	X			X	X	X			X	X		X	X			X	6
5	X			X	X				X	X			X			X	X				X	X			5
4			X	X			X			X	X				X	X			X			X	X		4
3	X			X	X				X	X			X			X	X				X	X			3
2	X	X			X	X		X	X			X	X	X			X	X		X	X			X	2
1	X	X	X			X	X	X			X	X	X	X	X			X	X	X			X	X	1
	24	23	22	21	20	19	18	17	16	15	14	13	12	11	10	9	8	7	6	5	4	3	2	1	

Chart 2

First round with steek stitches

Start knitting R 24 with the following partition (Chart 2):

» K the last 10 sts of the repeat (from st 15 up to and including st 24).
» Move SM.
» K the 24 sts of the central repeat.
» Move SM.
» K the last 9 sts of the repeat.
» Move SM to the right needle.
» K 14 steek sts according to the established colour scheme.
» Place SM.
» K the 15th steek st.

This first round with steek stitches does not feature any increase.

All following rounds

» K all sts according to Chart 2/R 1.
» At the end of this R, inc 1 st by kfb from the last st.
» Move SM to the right needle.
» K 14 steek sts.
» Move SM to the right needle.
» Inc 1 st by kfb from the 15th steek stitch

As increases are regularly added, the pattern must also be extended to the right and left.

For better orientation, each completed horizontal pattern repeat (pattern width) should be identified by the placement of SMs.

Once the first pattern repeat has been achieved hight-wise, start again with R 1.

In the end the shawl will be 292 rounds high (12 x 24 R of the complete pattern repeat plus one partial repeat from R 1 to and including R 4) and 578 sts wide.

The pattern is repeated 23 times horizontally in total (23 x 24 sts = 552 sts) plus the first 13 sts of a pattern repeat on the upper left tip and the last 13 sts of a pattern repeat on the upper right tip = 578 sts

Cutting the steek

Bind off steek sts 2 until 14 inclusive. Moisten and block the steek. When dry, secure the steek and cut it open.

Chart3

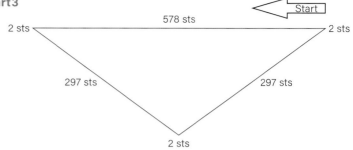

578 sts

2 sts   2 sts

297 sts   297 sts

2 sts

Version 1
BC = "magic ball" (terracotta)
PC = "magic ball" (turquoise)

Version 2
BC = "magic ball" (natural whites)
PC = "magic ball" (orange)

Border

K all 578 sts of the upper edge with BC.

Inc 1 st by kfb from the 1st steek st and place SM (left tip; 2-st-marker).
Pick up and knit 297 sts on the left side.
At the bottom tip inc 2 sts and place SM (2-st-marker).
Pick up and knit 297 sts on the right side.

Inc 1 st by kfb from the 15th steek st and place SM (right tip; 2-st-marker).

Purl one rd with BC (eyecatcher line).

At each of the 2-st-markers inc 1 st on both sides by M1R and M1L.

Each round will thus feature an increase of 6 sts.

Chart 4

R	24	23	22	21	20	19	18	17	16	15	14	13	12	11	10	9	8	7	6	5	4	3	2	1	R
18	FOLDING EDGE [PURL]																								18
17																		•							17
16			X							X						X						X			16
15		X	X	X					X	X	X				X	X	X				X	X	X		15
14			X							X						X						X			14
13	X						X						X						X						13
12	X	X					X	X	X				X	X	X				X	X	X			X	12
11	X						X						X						X						11
10			X							X						X						X			10
9		X	X	X					X	X	X				X	X	X				X	X	X		9
8			X							X						X						X			8
7	X						X						X						X						7
6	X	X					X	X	X				X	X	X				X	X	X			X	6
5	X						X						X						X						5
4			X							X						X						X			4
3		X	X	X					X	X	X				X	X	X				X	X	X		3
2			X							X						X						X			2
1																									1

BORDER PATTERN

R 1: k with BC.

The sts of the 2-st-markers are always knitted with BC.

Please be reminded to regularly increase (2-st-markers) at all three tips of the shawl. Due to the continuous increases, the pattern must also be extended to the left and the right.

R 2-16: k the border pattern with BC and PC.
R 17: k with BC only.
R 18: p with BC only (folding edge).
No increases are knitted at the three tips of the shawl.

Reverse side of the border

Now all increases previously made at the three tips of the shawl border front (2-st markers) must be decreased.

In each R before and after the 2-st-marker 1 st each has to be decreased left-leaning (ssk) and right-leaning (k2tog) accordingly.

This way 6 sts are being decreased in each round.

Please follow the pattern repeats as created for the front side of the border.

For the reverse side of the border please k R 17-1 of the border pattern.

Cast-off all sts and sew them to the inside of the border. See the description of the "knit-and-sew cast-off" method (cf. pages 24-26).

Finishing the shawl

Wash and block the shawl.
After drying the shawl, you might want to prepare tassels/pom-poms and sew them to the tips of the shawl together with felt balls.

GONDWANA

My knitting friend Melanie owns a chameleon called "Uncle Titus".
Melanie posted photos of him and I was thrilled to bits. Those colours!
And the colour idea for a new shawl appeared immediately!

Yarn

Abbreviation	Yarn Manufacturer	Yardage/100g
G	Gardiner S08 Shetland (100% wool)	450m/100g
G1	Gardiner SS11 Soft Shetland (100% wool)	565m/100g
H	Harrisville New England Shetland (100% pure wool)	397m/100g
J	Jamieson of Shetland Shetland Spindrift (100% pure Shetland wool)	420m/100g
JU	Jamieson of Shetland Ultra (50% Shetland/50% lambswool)	776m/100g
K	Knoll Supersoft (100% PURE NEW WOOL)	576m/100g
SF	Lankava Esito worsted wool yarn (100% wool)	425m/100g
Ra	Rauma Finull PT2 (100% Norwegian wool)	350m/100g
Re	Rennie Supersoft (100% lambswool)	565m/100g
ReU	Rennie Unique Shetland (100% lambswool)	450m/100g
ReC	Rennie Supersoft Cashmere (87.5% lambswool/12.5% cashmere)	492m/100g
LT	Tines 100% wool	350m/100g

Shetland Spindrift, Supersoft (lambswool), pure new wool etc. The yardage of the different yarns varies. Further information can be found in the chapter concerning yarns and suppliers (see pp. 160-161).

Version 1 "Turquoise-Green + Sand-Nature"

Yarn kit "Gondwana - Version 1" by Bärbel Salet VerstrickteKunst or

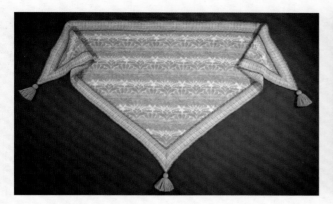

560 g pattern colour(s) (PC)
1 x 35 g Mint La (Re)
1 x 45 g Aquamarine (K)
1 x 50 g Marble Gemstone (Re)
1 x 60 g Apple (J)
3 x 70 g Seagreen (H), #435 Cyan (LT), Calypso (Re)*
2 x 80 g Grass (H)*, #454 Lime (Ra)*

400 g Background colour(s) (BC)
1 x 25 g Bracken (G)
3 x 35 g Wheatear (ReU), Camel (K), Almond (K)
2 x 40 g Sand (G), #8075 Sand (SF)
3 x 45 g Sand (J), Rye (J), Eesit (J)
1 x 55 g Laurel (ReU)

Piping cords: 45 g #8025 Orange (SF), 50 g Lelantos (ReC)

The amount of yarn required for the border and the tassels/pom-poms is included in the above.
*Tassels: Grass (H), Calypso (Re), #454 Lime (Ra)

Version 2 "Red-Red Orange + Anthracite"

(As depicted on p. 162, as well as on the front cover)

Yarn kit "Gondwana - Version 2" by Bärbel Salet VerstrickteKunst or

345 g pattern colour(s) (PC)
8 x 30 g Carmine (K), Queen of Heart (G), Scarlet (Re), Lelantos (ReC), Brandy (K), Tudor (Re), Scarlet (H), Crimson (J)
3 x 35 g Poppy (H), #424 Red (Ra), Red (H)

410 g background colour(s) (BC)
1 x 40 g Oxford (K)
5 x 50 g #8999 Black (SF), #8090 Graphite (SF), #8091 Dark grey (SF), Oxford (J), Graphite (K)*
2 x 60 g Charcoal (Re)*, Black (G)*

Piping cord: 35 g Amaranth Mix (Re), 60 g #8014 Magenta (SF)

210 g border pattern colour(s) (PC)
6 x 20 g Peony (K), Carnation (Re), Plum (J), #8014 Magenta (SF), #Dark Cherry (Ra), Lavish (Re)
1 x 25 g Pink (H)
1 x 30 g Raspberry (H)
1 x 35 g Elderberry (G)

The amount of yarn required for the border and the tassels/pom-poms is included in the above.

Tassels: Black (G), Charcoal (Re)*, Graphite

Arrangement of colours
Version 1

The colour scheme of BC and PC is knitted in a certain colour sequence; this can be found for both PC and BC in the right-hand columns of Charts 1 and 2 as well as for the border in Chart 5.

Version 2

The gradient colour schemes of both PC and BC are achieved with the help of previously prepared "magic balls", see the technical chapter, p. 13 ff. The wingspans are being determined individually. The border colour scheme for both PC and BC are mentioned in Chart 5.

Needles

3.25 mm circular needles (with different cable lengths); adjust needle size to obtain gauge if necessary.
DPNs might be useful at the beginning of the shawl.
3 sets of 3.25 mm circular needles with 100 cm cables for knitting the border; adjust needle size to obtain gauge if necessary.

Gauge

27 sts and 32 rows with 3.25 mm needles = 10 x 10 cm

Dimensions

Width 235 cm
Height 110 cm

Stitches

Stockinette stitch; two-colour Fair Isle knitting

Chart 1

	PC [x]	BC [ ]
23	Grass (H)	Laurel (ReU)
22	Grass (H)	Laurel (ReU)
21	Grass (H)	Laurel (ReU)
20	Grass (H)	Laurel (ReU)
19	Grass (H)	Rye (J)
18	Grass (H)	Rye (J)
17	Calypso (Re)	Rye (J)
16	Calypso (Re)	Rye (J)
15	Calypso (Re)	Rye (J)
14	Calypso (Re)	Rye (J)
13	Calypso (Re)	Eesit (J)
12	Calypso (Re)	Eesit (J)
11	Calypso (Re)	Eesit (J)
10	#454 Lime (Ra)	Eesit (J)
9	#454 Lime (Ra)	Eesit (J)
8	#454 Lime (Ra)	Eesit (J)
7	#454 Lime (Ra)	#8075 Sand (SF)
6	#454 Lime (Ra)	#8075 Sand (SF)
5	#454 Lime (Ra)	#8075 Sand (SF)
4		#8075 Sand (SF)
3		#8075 Sand (SF)
2		#8075 Sand (SF)
1		#8075 Sand (SF)

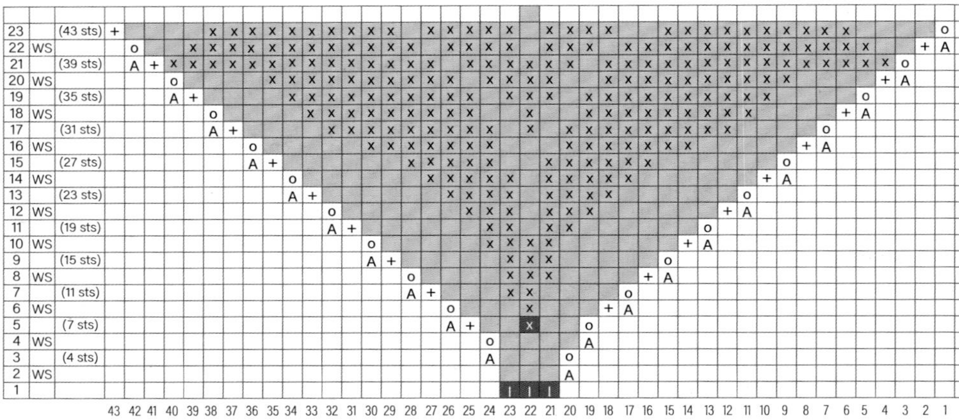

Legend:

- [x] pattern colour(s)
- [ ] background colour(s)
- [|] cast-on stitches
- [x] pattern starting point
- [A] chain cast-on stitch
- [o] knit
- [+] purl bump increase
- RS right side row
- WS wrong side row

Starting the shawl

R 1 cast-on row: co 3 sts with BC [|]

R 2 (WS): p 3 + chain cast-on 1 st [A]

R 3 (RS): k [o], k 3 sts = 4 sts, chain cast-on 1 st [A]

R 4 (WS): k [o], p 4 sts = 5 sts, chain cast-on 1 st [A]

R 5 (RS): This row marks the beginning/starting point of the patterned section. From this row onwards 1 st is increased each at the beginning [A] and at the end [+].

K R 6 (WS) up to and including R 23 (RS).

Integration of steek stitches

R 23 (RS/43 sts on needle): At the end of this row chain cast-on 15 steek sts, alternating between BC and PC. Close the row to a round. From now on all sts are k sts. Continue knitting either with DPNs or using the Magic Loop technique.

Please change to Chart 2 / R 24.

First round with steek stitches

Start knitting R 24 with the following partition (Chart 2):

» K from st 7 up to and including st 49.
» Place SM.
» K 14 steek sts according to the established colour scheme.
» Place SM.
» K the 15th steek st.

This first round with steek stitches does not feature any increase.

All following rounds

» K all sts according to Chart 2/R 25.
» At the end of this R, inc 1 st by kfb from the last st.
» Move SM to the right needle.
» K 14 steek sts.
» Move SM to the right needle.
» Inc 1 st by kfb from the 15th steek stitch

As increases are regularly added, the pattern must also be extended to the right and left.

For better orientation, completed horizontal pattern repeats should be identified by the placement of SMs.

Once the first pattern repeat has been achieved hight-wise, start again with R 1.

Chart 2

Column legend (columns 60 → 1):

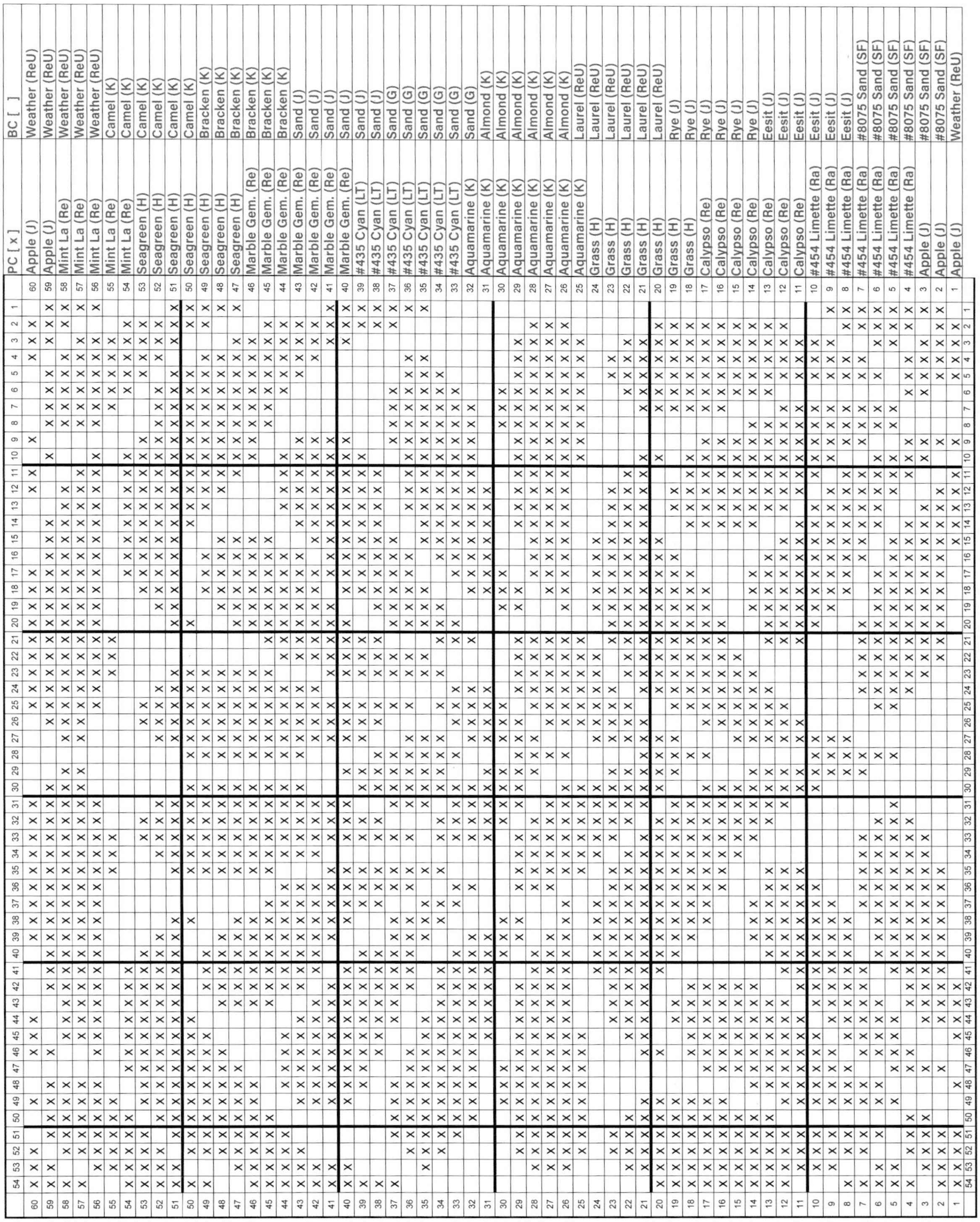

#	PC [x]	BC [ ]
60	Apple (J)	Weather (ReU)
59	Apple (J)	Weather (ReU)
58	Mint La (Re)	Weather (ReU)
57	Mint La (Re)	Weather (ReU)
56	Mint La (Re)	Weather (ReU)
55	Mint La (Re)	Camel (K)
54	Mint La (Re)	Camel (K)
53	Seagreen (H)	Camel (K)
52	Seagreen (H)	Camel (K)
51	Seagreen (H)	Camel (K)
50	Seagreen (H)	Bracken (K)
49	Seagreen (H)	Bracken (K)
48	Seagreen (H)	Bracken (K)
47	Seagreen (H)	Bracken (K)
46	Marble Gem. (Re)	Bracken (K)
45	Marble Gem. (Re)	Bracken (K)
44	Marble Gem. (Re)	Bracken (K)
43	Marble Gem. (Re)	Sand (J)
42	Marble Gem. (Re)	Sand (J)
41	Marble Gem. (Re)	Sand (J)
40	#435 Cyan (LT)	Sand (J)
39	#435 Cyan (LT)	Sand (G)
38	#435 Cyan (LT)	Sand (G)
37	#435 Cyan (LT)	Sand (G)
36	#435 Cyan (LT)	Sand (G)
35	#435 Cyan (LT)	Sand (G)
34	#435 Cyan (LT)	Sand (G)
33	#435 Cyan (LT)	Almond (K)
32	Aquamarine (K)	Almond (K)
31	Aquamarine (K)	Almond (K)
30	Aquamarine (K)	Almond (K)
29	Aquamarine (K)	Almond (K)
28	Aquamarine (K)	Almond (K)
27	Aquamarine (K)	Laurel (ReU)
26	Aquamarine (K)	Laurel (ReU)
25	Grass (H)	Laurel (ReU)
24	Grass (H)	Laurel (ReU)
23	Grass (H)	Laurel (ReU)
22	Grass (H)	Rye (J)
21	Grass (H)	Rye (J)
20	Grass (H)	Rye (J)
19	Calypso (Re)	Rye (J)
18	Calypso (Re)	Rye (J)
17	Calypso (Re)	Eesit (J)
16	Calypso (Re)	Eesit (J)
15	Calypso (Re)	Eesit (J)
14	Calypso (Re)	Eesit (J)
13	Calypso (Re)	Eesit (J)
12	#454 Limette (Ra)	Eesit (J)
11	#454 Limette (Ra)	#8075 Sand (SF)
10	#454 Limette (Ra)	#8075 Sand (SF)
9	#454 Limette (Ra)	#8075 Sand (SF)
8	#454 Limette (Ra)	#8075 Sand (SF)
7	#454 Limette (Ra)	#8075 Sand (SF)
6		#8075 Sand (SF)
5		#8075 Sand (SF)
4		Apple (J)
3		Apple (J)
2		Apple (J)
1		Weather (ReU)

In the end the shawl will be 294 rounds high (4 x 60 R of the complete pattern repeat plus one partial repeat from R 1 to and including R 54) and 582 sts wide.

The pattern is repeated 9 times horizontally in total (9 x 54 sts = 486 sts) plus the first 48 sts of a pattern repeat on the upper left tip and the last 48 sts of a pattern repeat on the upper right tip = 582 sts.

Cutting the steek

Bind off steek sts 2 until 14 inclusive. Moisten and block the steek. When dry, secure the steek and cut it open.

Border

Version 1
BC = see Chart 5
PC = see Chart 5

Version 2
BC = "magic ball"
(black-anthracite)
PC = see Chart 5

Piping cord colours

Version 1
Lelantos (ReC)
#8025 Orange (SF)

Version 2
Amaranth Mix (Re)
#8014 Magenta (SF)

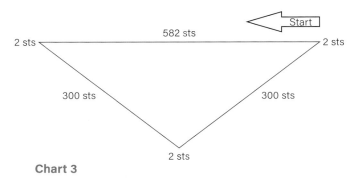

Chart 3

Piping cord pattern

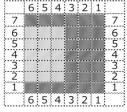 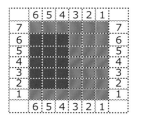

Chart 4.1 - Version 1   **Chart 4.2 - Version 2**

Chart 4.1 or Chart 4.2

R 1:
K all 582 sts of the upper edge with Lelantos (ReC) for Version 1 or #8014 Magenta (SF) for Version 2 with 3.25 mm needles.

Inc 1 st by kfb from the 1st steek st and place SM (left tip; 2-st-marker).
Pick up and knit 300 sts on the left side.
At the bottom tip inc 2 sts and place SM (2-st-marker).
Pick up and knit 300 sts on the right side.

Inc 1 st by kfb from the 15th steek st and place SM (right tip; 2-st-marker).

R 2-6:
K the piping cord pattern with 3.25 mm needles; adjust needle size to obtain gauge if necessary.
The sts of the 2-st-markers are knit with 1 st each in the colours as mentioned. All these rounds do not feature any increases.

Forming the piping cord

Chart 4.1 or Chart 4.2:
R 7: K with Lelantos (ReC) for Version 1 or #8014 Magenta (SF) for Version 2 and knit each and every stitch together with the corresponding stitch of R 1 on the reverse side of the border. This round does not feature any increases.

BORDER PATTERN

At each of the 2-st-markers inc 1 st on both sides by M1R and M1L.

R 1: k with PC as per Chart 5

The sts of the 2-st-markers are always knitted with PC.

Please be reminded to regularly increase (2-st-markers) at all three tips of the shawl.

Due to the continuous increases, the pattern must also be extended to the left and the right.

R 2-27: k the border pattern with BC and PC according to Chart 5.
R 28: k with BC only according to Chart 5
R 29-34: k the piping cord pattern (without any increases).

Forming the outer piping cord:
R 35: K each and every stitch together with the corresponding stitch of R 29 on the reverse side of the border.
This round does not feature any increases.

Reverse side of the border

Now all increases previously made at the three tips of the shawl border front (2-st markers) must be decreased.

In each R before and after the 2-st-marker 1 st each has to be decreased left-leaning (ssk) and right-leaning (k2tog) accordingly.

This way 6 sts are being decreased in each round.

Please follow the pattern repeats as created for the front side of the border.

BORDER PATTERN

Chart5

Stitch chart (columns 18–1):

18	17	16	15	14	13	12	11	10	9	8	7	6	5	4	3	2	1	R
X	X	X	X	X	X	X	X	X	X	X	X	X	X	X	X	X	X	63
X						X					X							62
X						X					X							61
X	X	X	X	X	X	X	X	X	X	X	X	X	X	X	X	X	X	60
X						X					X							59
X						X					X							58
X	X	X	X	X	X	X	X	X	X	X	X	X	X	X	X	X	X	57
X						X					X							56
X						X					X							55
X	X	X	X	X	X	X	X	X	X	X	X	X	X	X	X	X	X	54
X						X					X							53
X						X					X							52
X	X	X	X	X	X	X	X	X	X	X	X	X	X	X	X	X	X	51
X						X					X							50
X						X					X							49
X	X	X	X	X	X	X	X	X	X	X	X	X	X	X	X	X	X	48
X						X					X							47
X						X					X							46
X	X	X	X	X	X	X	X	X	X	X	X	X	X	X	X	X	X	45
X						X					X							44
X						X					X							43
X	X	X	X	X	X	X	X	X	X	X	X	X	X	X	X	X	X	42
X						X					X							41
X						X					X							40
X	X	X	X	X	X	X	X	X	X	X	X	X	X	X	X	X	X	39
X						X					X							38
X						X					X							37
X	X	X	X	X	X	X	X	X	X	X	X	X	X	X	X	X	X	36
																		35
																		34
																		33
																		32
																		31
																		30
																		29
X	X	X	X	X	X	X	X	X	X	X	X	X	X	X	X	X	X	28
X						X					X							27
X						X					X							26
X	X	X	X	X	X	X	X	X	X	X	X	X	X	X	X	X	X	25
X						X					X							24
X						X					X							23
X	X	X	X	X	X	X	X	X	X	X	X	X	X	X	X	X	X	22
X						X					X							21
X						X					X							20
X	X	X	X	X	X	X	X	X	X	X	X	X	X	X	X	X	X	19
X						X					X							18
X						X					X							17
X	X	X	X	X	X	X	X	X	X	X	X	X	X	X	X	X	X	16
X						X					X							15
X						X					X							14
X	X	X	X	X	X	X	X	X	X	X	X	X	X	X	X	X	X	13
X						X					X							12
X						X					X							11
X	X	X	X	X	X	X	X	X	X	X	X	X	X	X	X	X	X	10
X						X					X							9
X						X					X							8
X	X	X	X	X	X	X	X	X	X	X	X	X	X	X	X	X	X	7
X						X					X							6
X						X					X							5
X	X	X	X	X	X	X	X	X	X	X	X	X	X	X	X	X	X	4
X						X					X							3
X						X					X							2
X	X	X	X	X	X	X	X	X	X	X	X	X	X	X	X	X	X	1

Colours:

R	Version 1 — PC [x]	Version 1 — BC [ ]	Version 2 — PC [x]
63	Apple (J)		Peony (K)
62	Apple (J)	Wheatear (ReU)	Peony (K)
61	Apple (J)	Wheatear (ReU)	Peony (K)
60	Apple (J)		Carnation (Re)
59	Mint La (Re)	Camel (K)	Carnation (Re)
58	Mint La (Re)	Camel (K)	Carnation (Re)
57	Mint La (Re)		Plum (J)
56	Seagreen (H)	Sand (J)	Plum (J)
55	Seagreen (H)	Sand (J)	Plum (J)
54	Seagreen (H)		#8014 Magenta (SF)
53	Marble Gemstone (Re)	Sand (G)	#8014 Magenta (SF)
52	Marble Gemstone (Re)	Sand (G)	#8014 Magenta (SF)
51	Marble Gemstone (Re)		#4886 Pink (Ra)
50	#435 Cyan (LT)	Almond (K)	#4886 Pink (Ra)
49	#435 Cyan (LT)	Almond (K)	#4886 Pink (Ra)
48	#435 Cyan (LT)		Pink (H)
47	Aquamarine (K)	Laurel (ReU)	Pink (H)
46	Aquamarine (K)	Laurel (ReU)	Pink (H)
45	Aquamarine (K)		Raspberry (H)
44	Grass (H)	Rye (J)	Raspberry (H)
43	Grass (H)	Rye (J)	Raspberry (H)
42	Grass (H)		Lavish (Re)
41	Calypso (Re)	Eesit (J)	Lavish (Re)
40	Calypso (Re)	Eesit (J)	Lavish (Re)
39	Calypso (Re)		Elderberry (G)
38	#454 Lime (Ra)	#8075 Sand (SF)	Elderberry (G)
37	#454 Lime (Ra)	#8075 Sand (SF)	Elderberry (G)
36	#454 Lime (Ra)		Elderberry (G)
35	Chart#4.1		Chart#4.2
34	Chart#4.1		Chart#4.2
33	Chart#4.1		Chart#4.2
32	Chart#4.1		Chart#4.2
31	Chart#4.1		Chart#4.2
30	Chart#4.1		Chart#4.2
29	Chart#4.1		Chart#4.2
28	Apple (J)		Elderberry (G)
27	Apple (J)	Wheatear (ReU)	Elderberry (G)
26	Apple (J)	Wheatear (ReU)	Elderberry (G)
25	Apple (J)		Elderberry (G)
24	Mint La (Re)	Camel (K)	Lavish (Re)
23	Mint La (Re)	Camel (K)	Lavish (Re)
22	Mint La (Re)		Lavish (Re)
21	Seagreen (H)	Sand (J)	Raspberry (H)
20	Seagreen (H)	Sand (J)	Raspberry (H)
19	Seagreen (H)		Raspberry (H)
18	Marble Gemstone (Re)	Sand (G)	Pink (H)
17	Marble Gemstone (Re)	Sand (G)	Pink (H)
16	Marble Gemstone (Re)		Pink (H)
15	#435 Cyan (LT)	Almond (K)	#4886 Hot Pink (Ra)
14	#435 Cyan (LT)	Almond (K)	#4886 Hot Pink (Ra)
13	#435 Cyan (LT)		#4886 Hot Pink (Ra)
12	Aquamarine (K)	Laurel (ReU)	#8014 Magenta (SF)
11	Aquamarine (K)	Laurel (ReU)	#8014 Magenta (SF)
10	Aquamarine (K)		#8014 Magenta (SF)
9	Grass (H)	Rye (J)	Plum (J)
8	Grass (H)	Rye (J)	Plum (J)
7	Grass (H)		Plum (J)
6	Calypso (Re)	Eesit (J	Carnation (Re)
5	Calypso (Re)	Eesit (J	Carnation (Re)
4	Calypso (Re)		Carnation (Re)
3	#454 Limette (Ra)	#8075 Sand (SF)	Peony (K)
2	#454 Limette (Ra)	#8075 Sand (SF)	Peony (K)
1	#454 Limette (Ra)		Peony (K)

R 36: k with BC only according to Chart 5.
R 37-62: k the border pattern with PC according to Chart 5.

Rd 63: k with BC only / cast-off all stitches and sew them to the inside of the border. See the description of the "knit-and-sew cast-off" method (cf. pages 24-26).

Finishing the shawl

Wash and block the shawl. After drying the shawl, you might want to prepare tassels/pom-poms.

Play Of The Seasons

The name "Play of the Seasons" stands for the versatility of all colours. The original version of this shawl I knitted in winter colours, but I can also imagine the shawl to be knit in summer, spring or autumn colours. This shawl offers so many possibilities to indulge in your own and individual colour scheme!

Yarn

Abbreviation	Yarn Manufacturer	Yardage/100g
G	Gardiner S08 Shetland (100% wool)	450m/100g
G1	Gardiner SS11 Soft Shetland (100% wool)	565m/100g
H	Harrisville New England Shetland (100% pure wool)	397m/100g
J	Jamieson of Shetland Shetland Spindrift (100% pure Shetland wool)	420m/100g
K	Knoll Supersoft (100% PURE NEW WOOL)	576m/100g
SF	Lankava Esito worsted wool yarn (100% wool)	425m/100g
Re	Rennie Supersoft (100% lambswool)	565m/100g
LT	Tines 100% wool	350m/100g

Shetland Spindrift, Supersoft (lambswool), pure new wool etc. The yardage of the different yarns varies. Further information can be found in the chapter concerning yarns and suppliers (see pp. 160-161).

Version 1 "Turquoise-Seagreen + Petrol-Dark Blue"

Yarn kit "Play of the Seasons - Version 1" by Bärbel Salet VerstrickteKunst or

380 g pattern colour(s) (PC)

14 x 25 g Kingfisher (K), Verdigris (J), Seagreen (H), Marble Gemstone (Re), #435 Cyan (LT), Aquamarine (K), Mineral Blue (G), Caspian (J), Aegean (H), Seabright (J), Azure (Re), Neptune (G1), Peacock (H), Mermaid (J)
30 g Splash (J) - also for e.g., the eyecatcher line

420 g background colour(s) (BC)

6 x 70 g Midnight (G), Vintage Heather (K), Mariner (K), Indigo (K), Midnight (J), Denim (Re)

The amount of yarn required for the border and the pom-poms is included in the above.

Version 2 "Pastel Shades + Light Green-Citreous"

Yarn kit "Play of the Seasons - Version 2" by Bärbel Salet VerstrickteKunst or

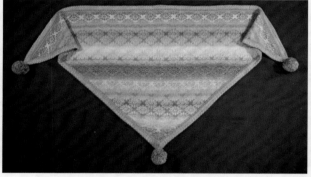

380 g pattern colour(s) (PC)

7 x 15 g Geranium (K), Rosebud (K), Dog Rose (J), Strawberry Sherbet (Re), Sugarsnape (K), Sunglow (J), Perfect Peach (Re)
10 x 20 g Salmon (Re), Sorbet (J), Allium (K), Heather Orchid (Re), Pink Lavender (G), #250 Lilac (LT), Orchid (J), Rose (J), Peach (J), Flame (J)
3 x 25 g Water Lily (H), #522 Flamingo (LT), Apricot (J)

390 g background colour(s) (BC)

6 x 35 g Pea Green (K), Apple (J), Fig Leaf (G1), #8041 Green (SF), Mint La (Re), #8041 Leaf Green (SF)
6 x 30 g Calypso (K), Stonehenge (Re), #8037 Pistachio (SF), Lime (H), Lime Sorbet (Re), Spring Meadow (Re)

Eyecatcher line
30 g Tangerine (J)

The amount of yarn required for the border and the pom-poms is included in the above.

		8	7	6	5	4	3	2	1	28	27	26	25	24	23	22	21	20	19	18	17	16	15	14	13	12	11	10	9	8	7	6	5	4	3	2	1	28	27	26	25	24	23	22			
23		(43 M)	+		x	x	x		x	x	x		x	x	x				x	x		x	x	x		x	x			x	x				x	x	x		x	x	x		x	x	x		o			HR	23
22	RR			o	x	x	x	x		x	x	x	x				x	x	x		x	x	x		x	x	x	x				x	x	x	x		x		x	x	x	x	+	A	(41 M)			22
21		(39 M)	A	+	x	x		x	x	x		x	x					x	x		x	x		x	x	x		x	x	x			x	x		x	x	x		x	x	o				HR	21
20	RR				o		x	x	x				x	x	x	x		x	x		x	x		x	x		x	x	x		x	x	x			x	x	x		+	A	(37 M)				20
19		(35 M)		A	+		x				x	x	x	x		x	x		x	x		x	x		x	x	x	x	x			x		o			+	A					HR	19
18	RR				o					x		x	x	x		x		x			x	x	x		x			+	A	(33 M)													18
17		(31 M)			A	+					x		x	x	x		x		x	x	x		x			o		+	A													HR	17
16	RR					o			x	x		x	x		x	x	x	x		x	x		x	x		x	x			+	A	(29 M)												16
15		(27 M)				A	+		x	x	x	x	x		x	x	x		x	x		x	x	x	x	x		o														HR	15
14	RR					o		x	x		x	x		x	x	x	x		x	x		x	x		+	A	(25 M)																14
13		(23 M)				A	+		x		x	x	x		x		x	x	x		x		o																	HR	13
12	RR					o	x		x	x	x		x		x		x	x	x		x	+	A	(21 M)																		12
11		(19 M)				A	+	x	x	x	x		x	x		x		x	x	x	x	o																			HR	11
10	RR					o	x	x		x	x		x	x	x		x	x	+	A	(17 M)																					10
9		(15 M)				A	+	x	x	x		x	x	x		x	x	x	o																					HR	9
8	RR					o	x	x	x	x		x	x	x	x	+	A	(13 M)																							8
7		(11 M)				A	+	x	x		x	x	x		x	x	o																							HR	7
6	RR					o		x	x	x		+	A	(9 M)																										6
5		(7 M)				A	+		x		o																												HR	5
4	RR					o			A	(5 M)																														4
3		(4 M)				A		o																															HR	3
2	RR						A																																	2
1							∎	∎	∎																														HR	1

Chart 1   43 42 41 40 39 38 37 36 35 34 33 32 31 30 29 28 27 26 25 24 23 22 21 20 19 18 17 16 15 14 13 12 11 10 9 8 7 6 5 4 3 2 1

x	pattern colour(s)		∎	cast-on stitches		A	chain cast-on stitch	RS	right side row
	background colour(s)		x	pattern starting point		o	knit	WS	wrong side row
						+	purl bump increase	

Arrangement of colours Version 1 and Version 2

The gradient colour schemes of both PC and BC are achieved with the help of previously prepared "magic balls", see the technical chapter, p. 13 ff. The wingspans are being determined individually.

Needles

3.25 mm circular needles (with different cable lengths); adjust needle size to obtain gauge if necessary.
DPNs might be useful at the beginning of the shawl.
3 sets of 3.25 mm circular needles with 100 cm cables for knitting the border; adjust needle size to obtain gauge if necessary.

Gauge

27 sts and 32 rows with 3.25 mm needles = 10 x 10 cm

Dimensions

Width 234 cm
Height 99 cm

Stitches

Stockinette stitch; two-colour Fair Isle knitting

Starting the shawl

R 1 cast-on row: co 3 sts with BC [|]
R 2 (WS): p 3 + chain cast-on 1 st [A]
R 3 (RS): k [o], k 3 sts = 4 sts, chain cast-on 1 st [A]
R 4 (WS): k [o], p 4 sts = 5 sts, chain cast-on 1 st [A]
R 5 (RS): This row marks the beginning/starting point of the patterned section. From this row onwards 1 st is increased each at the beginning [A] and at the end [+].
K R 6 (WS) up to and including R 23 (RS) acc. to Chart 1.

TIP: In row 17, new repeats begin on both the left and right side of the central repeat. Mark these with SMs.

Integration of steek stitches

R 23 (RS/43 sts on needle): At the end of this row chain cast-on 15 steek sts, alternating between BC and PC. Close the row to a round. From now on all sts are k sts. Continue knitting either with DPNs or using the Magic Loop technique.

Please change to Chart 2 / R 24.

	28	27	26	25	24	23	22	21	20	19	18	17	16	15	14	13	12	11	10	9	8	7	6	5	4	3	2	1	
28	X	X				X	X		X	X								X	X		X	X				X	X	X	28
27		X	X	X			X													X			X	X	X		X		27
26	X			X	X	X			X											X			X	X	X		X		26
25		X	X		X	X	X	X	X					X					X	X	X	X	X		X	X		X	25
24	X		X	X		X	X	X					X	X	X					X	X	X		X	X		X	X	24
23	X		X	X	X					X	X		X	X	X		X	X				X	X	X			X	X	23
22		X	X	X	X				X	X	X	X		X		X	X	X				X	X	X	X		X		22
21	X		X	X					X	X	X		X	X	X		X	X				X	X			X	X		21
20	X				X	X	X			X	X		X	X	X		X	X	X	X	X						X	X	20
19				X	X	X	X		X		X	X		X		X	X		X	X	X	X	X				X		19
18			X						X	X	X		X		X		X	X	X		X								18
17			X						X	X	X		X			X	X	X			X								17
16				X	X		X	X					X	X	X	X	X		X	X			X	X					16
15			X	X	X	X	X	X	X		X	X	X			X	X	X	X	X	X	X	X	X	X				15
14			X	X			X	X			X	X	X	X	X				X	X			X	X					14
13				X					X	X	X		X			X	X	X		X									13
12					X	X			X	X	X		X		X		X	X	X		X								12
11				X	X	X	X	X	X		X	X		X		X	X	X	X	X	X	X	X					X	11
10	X				X	X	X		X	X		X	X	X		X	X	X	X	X							X	X	10
9	X		X	X					X	X	X		X	X	X		X	X	X				X	X			X	X	9
8		X	X	X	X				X	X	X	X		X		X	X	X	X				X	X	X	X		X	8
7	X		X	X	X				X	X			X	X	X		X	X					X	X	X		X	X	7
6	X		X	X		X	X	X					X	X	X					X	X	X		X	X		X	X	6
5		X	X		X	X	X	X	X				X						X	X	X	X	X		X	X		X	5
4	X			X	X	X			X											X		X	X	X		X			4
3		X	X	X				X												X		X	X	X			X		3
2	X	X			X	X			X	X								X	X		X	X				X	X	X	2
1	X	X	X		X	X	X	X	X	X	X				X	X	X	X	X	X	X	X	X	X		X	X		1
	28	27	26	25	24	23	22	21	20	19	18	17	16	15	14	13	12	11	10	9	8	7	6	5	4	3	2	1	

Chart 2

First round with steek stitches

Start knitting R 24 with the following partition (Chart 2):

» K the last 7 sts of the repeat (from st 22 up to and including st 28).
» Move SM.
» K the 28 sts of the central repeat.
» Move SM.
» K the first 8 sts of the repeat.
» Move SM to the right needle.
» K 14 steek sts according to the established colour scheme.
» Place SM.
» K the 15th steek st.

This first round with steek stitches does not feature any increase.

All following rounds

» K all sts according to Chart 2/R 25.
» At the end of this R, inc 1 st by kfb from the last st.
» Move SM to the right needle.
» K 14 steek sts.
» Move SM to the right needle.
» Inc 1 st by kfb from the 15th steek stitch

As increases are regularly added, the pattern must also be extended to the right and left.

For better orientation, completed horizontal pattern repeats should be identified by the placement of SMs.

Once the first pattern repeat has been achieved hight-wise, start again with R 1.

In the end the shawl will be 296 rounds high (10 x 28 R of the complete pattern repeat plus one partial repeat from R 1 to and including R 15 plus one R with BC only) and 586 sts wide.

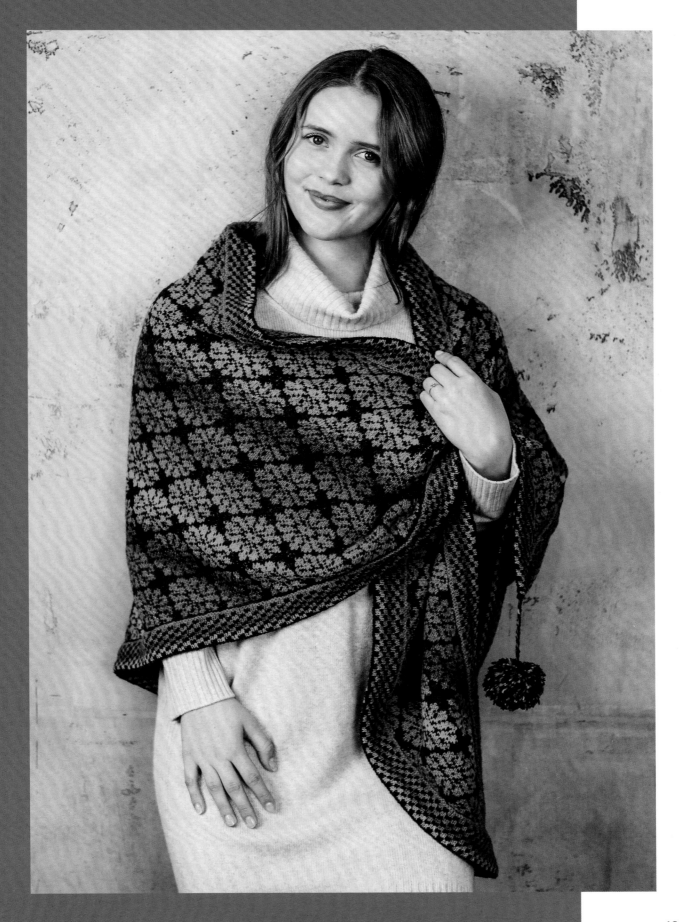

The pattern is repeated 19 times horizontally in total (19 x 28 sts = 532 sts) plus the first 26 sts of a pattern repeat on the upper left tip plus 1 st from R 296 = 27 sts and the last 26 sts of a pattern repeat on the upper right tip plus 1 st from R 296 = 27 sts.
Total = 586 sts.

Cutting the steek

Bind off steek sts 2 until 14 inclusive. Moisten and block the steek. When dry, secure the steek and cut it open.

Border

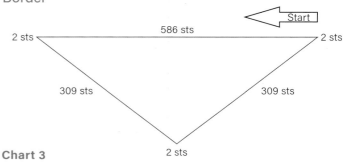

Chart 3

Version 1
BC = "magic ball"
(petrol-midnight)
PC = see Chart 4

Version 2
BC = "magic ball"
(green-citreous)
PC = "magic ball"
(pastel shades)

K all 586 sts of the upper edge with Splash (J) for Version 1 or Tangerine (J) for Version 2.

Inc 1 st by kfb from the 1st steek st and place SM (left tip; 2-st-marker).
Pick up and knit 309 sts on the left side.
At the bottom tip inc 2 sts and place SM (2-st-marker).
Pick up and knit 309 sts on the right side.

Inc 1 st by kfb from the 15th steek st and place SM (right tip; 2-st-marker).

Purl one rd with Splash (J) for Version 1 or Tangerine (J) for Version 2 (eyecatcher line).

At each of the 2-st-markers inc 1 st on both sides by M1R and M1L.

Each round will thus feature an increase of 6 sts.

BORDER PATTERN

Variante 1

	20	19	18	17	16	15	14	13	12	11	10	9	8	7	6	5	4	3	2	1		PC [x]
31																					31	
30		X	X		X	X		X	X		X	X		X	X		X	X		X	30	Kingfisher (K)
29		X	X		X	X		X	X		X	X		X	X		X	X		X	29	Kingfisher (K)
28	X	X		X	X		X	X		X	X		X	X		X	X		X	X	28	Azure (Re)
27	X	X		X	X		X	X		X	X		X	X		X	X		X	X	27	Azure (Re)
26		X	X		X	X		X	X		X	X		X	X		X	X		X	26	Seabright (J)
25		X	X		X	X		X	X		X	X		X	X		X	X		X	25	Seabright (J)
24	X	X		X	X		X	X		X	X		X	X		X	X		X	X	24	Aegean (H)
23	X	X		X	X		X	X		X	X		X	X		X	X		X	X	23	Aegean (H)
22		X	X		X	X		X	X		X	X		X	X		X	X		X	22	Caspian (J)
21		X	X		X	X		X	X		X	X		X	X		X	X		X	21	Caspian (J)
20	X	X		X	X		X	X		X	X		X	X		X	X		X	X	20	Mineral Blue (G)
19	X	X		X	X		X	X		X	X		X	X		X	X		X	X	19	Mineral Blue (G)
18		X	X		X	X		X	X		X	X		X	X		X	X		X	18	Aquamarine (K)
17		X	X		X	X		X	X		X	X		X	X		X	X		X	17	Aquamarine (K)
16					FOLDING EDGE [PURL]																16	
15																					15	
14		X	X		X	X		X	X		X	X		X	X		X	X		X	14	Marble Gemstone (Re)
13		X	X		X	X		X	X		X	X		X	X		X	X		X	13	Marble Gemstone (Re)
12	X	X		X	X		X	X		X	X		X	X		X	X		X	X	12	Seagreen (H)
11	X	X		X	X		X	X		X	X		X	X		X	X		X	X	11	Seagreen (H)
10		X	X		X	X		X	X		X	X		X	X		X	X		X	10	Verdigris (J)
9		X	X		X	X		X	X		X	X		X	X		X	X		X	9	Verdigris (J)
8	X	X		X	X		X	X		X	X		X	X		X	X		X	X	8	Mermaid (J)
7	X	X		X	X		X	X		X	X		X	X		X	X		X	X	7	Mermaid (J)
6		X	X		X	X		X	X		X	X		X	X		X	X		X	6	Peacock (H)
5		X	X		X	X		X	X		X	X		X	X		X	X		X	5	Peacock (H)
4	X	X		X	X		X	X		X	X		X	X		X	X		X	X	4	Neptune (G)
3	X	X		X	X		X	X		X	X		X	X		X	X		X	X	3	Neptune (G)
2		X	X		X	X		X	X		X	X		X	X		X	X		X	2	Azure (Re)
1		X	X		X	X		X	X		X	X		X	X		X	X		X	1	Azure (Re)
	20	19	18	17	16	15	14	13	12	11	10	9	8	7	6	5	4	3	2	1		

Chart4

The sts of the 2-st-markers are always knitted with BC. Please be reminded to regularly increase (2-st-markers) at all three tips of the shawl. Due to the continuous increases, the pattern must also be extended to the left and the right.

R 1-14: k the border pattern with BC and PC according to Chart 4.
R 15: k with BC only.
R 16: p with the yarn colour according to Chart 4 (folding edge). No increases are knitted at the three tips of the shawl.

Reverse side of the border

Now all increases previously made at the three tips of the shawl border front (2-st markers) must be decreased.

In each R before and after the 2-st-marker 1 st each has to be decreased left-leaning (ssk) and right-leaning (k2tog) accordingly.

This way 6 sts are being decreased in each round. Please follow the pattern repeats as created for the front side of the border.

R 17-30: k the border pattern with PC according to Chart 4.
R 31: k with BC only.

Cast-off all sts and sew them to the inside of the border. See the description of the "knit-and-sew cast-off" method (see pp. 24-26).

Finishing the shawl

Wash and block the shawl.

After drying the shawl, you might want to prepare tassels/pom-poms and sew them to the tips of the shawl.

RISE LIKE A PHOENIX

The pattern reminds me of the colourful plumage of a bird.
The many colour possibilities let one's imagination run wild!

Yarn

Abbreviation	Yarn Manufacturer	Yardage/100g
G	Gardiner S08 Shetland (100% wool)	450m/100g
G1	Gardiner SS11 Soft Shetland (100% wool)	565m/100g
H	Harrisville New England Shetland (100% pure wool)	397m/100g
J	Jamieson of Shetland Shetland Spindrift (100% pure Shetland wool)	420m/100g
JU	Jamieson of Shetland Ultra (50% Shetland/50% lambswool)	776m/100g
K	Knoll Supersoft (100% PURE NEW WOOL)	576m/100g
SF	Lankava Esito worsted wool yarn (100% wool)	425m/100g
Ra	Rauma Finull PT2 (100% Norwegian wool)	350m/100g
Re	Rennie Supersoft (100% lambswool)	565m/100g
ReU	Rennie Unique Shetland (100% lambswool)	450m/100g
ReC	Rennie Supersoft Cashmere (87.5% lambswool/ 12.5% cashmere)	492m/100g
LT	Tines 100% wool	350m/100g

Shetland Spindrift, Supersoft (lambswool), pure new wool etc. The yardage of the different yarns varies. Further information can be found in the chapter concerning yarns and suppliers (see pp. 160-161).

Version 1 "Atlantic + Light Blue"

Yarn kit "Rise Like a Phoenix - Version 1" by Bärbel Salet VerstrickteKunst or:

490 g pattern colour(s) (PC)
7 x 70 g Iced (K), Powder Blue (ReC), Porcelain (ReU), Surf (J), Duck Egg (Re), Sky (G), Cornflower (K)

420 g background colour(s) (BC)
Atlantic Spray (Re)

The amount of yarn required for the border and (optional) tassels/pom-poms is included in the above.

Version 2 "Berry Shades Fuchsia-Orange-Apricot-Pink + Blue-Green-Citreous"

Yarn kit "Rise Like a Phoenix - Version 2" by Bärbel Salet VerstrickteKunst or:

460 g pattern colour(s) (PC)
8 x 15 g Tangerine (J), Clementine (K), Pumpkin (J), Spice (Re), Poppy (H), Scarlet (Re), Peony (K), Allium (K)
7 x 20 g Scarlet (J), Red (H), Crimson (J), Cherry (J), Chianti (H), Sugarsnape (K), Apricot (J)
2 x 35 g *Elderberry (G), *Carnation (Re)
1 x 40 g *Raspberry (H)
2 x 45 g *Plum (J), *Pink (H)

540 g background colour(s) (BC)
15 x 15 g Kingfisher (K), Verdigris (J), Seagreen (H), #8041 Green (SF), Kiwi (H), New Lawn (Re), Leprechaun (J), Garden Leaf (Re), Calypso (Re), Grass (H), Calypso (K), Stonehenge (Re), Spring Meadow (Re), Dewdrop (J), Surf (J)
1 x 50 g *Azure (Re)
1 x 55 g *Seabright (J)

Knitting chart (Chart 1). Column numbers across top: 5 4 3 2 1 33 32 31 30 29 28 27 26 25 24 23 22 21 20 19 18 17 16 15 14 13 12 11 10 9 8 7 6 5 4 3 2 1 33 32 31 30 29. Bottom numbers: 43 42 41 40 39 38 37 36 35 34 33 32 31 30 29 28 27 26 25 24 23 22 21 20 19 18 17 16 15 14 13 12 11 10 9 8 7 6 5 4 3 2 1.

Row	sts	sts	RS/WS	Version 1 PC [X]	Version 1 PC [X]	Version 2 BC [ ]
23	(43 sts)		RS	Porcelain (ReU)	Poppy (H)	Kiwi (H)
22 WS		(41 sts)		Porcelain (ReU)	Poppy (H)	Kiwi (H)
21	(39 sts)		RS	Porcelain (ReU)	Poppy (H)	Kiwi (H)
20 WS		(37 sts)		Porcelain (ReU)	Spice (Re)	#8041 Green (SF)
19	(35 sts)		RS	Porcelain (ReU)	Spice (Re)	#8041 Green (SF)
18 WS		(33 sts)		Porcelain (ReU)	Spice (Re)	#8041 Green (SF)
17	(31 sts)		RS	Porcelain (ReU)	Spice (Re)	#8041 Green (SF)
16 WS		(29 sts)		Powder Blue (ReC)	Spice (Re)	#8041 Green (SF)
15	(27 sts)		RS	Powder Blue (ReC)	Pumpkin (J)	Seagreen (H)
14 WS		(25 sts)		Powder Blue (ReC)	Pumpkin (J)	Seagreen (H)
13	(23 sts)		RS	Powder Blue (ReC)	Pumpkin (J)	Seagreen (H)
12 WS		(21 sts)		Powder Blue (ReC)	Pumpkin (J)	Seagreen (H)
11	(19 sts)		RS	Powder Blue (ReC)	Pumpkin (J)	Seagreen (H)
10 WS		(17 sts)		Powder Blue (ReC)	Clementine (K)	Verdigris (J)
9	(15 sts)		RS	Powder Blue (ReC)	Clementine (K)	Verdigris (J)
8 WS		(13 sts)		Iced (K)	Clementine (K)	Verdigris (J)
7	(11 sts)		RS	Iced (K)	Clementine (K)	Verdigris (J)
6 WS		(9 sts)		Iced (K)	Clementine (K)	Verdigris (J)
5	(7 sts)		RS	Iced (K)	Tangerine (J)	Kingfisher (K)
4 WS		(5 sts)				Kingfisher (K)
3	(4 sts)		RS			Kingfisher (K)
2 WS						Kingfisher (K)
1			RS			Kingfisher (K)

Legend:

- x pattern colour(s)
-    background colour(s)
- ▮ cast-on stitches
- x pattern starting point
- A chain cast-on stitch
- o knit
- + purl bump increase
- RS right side row
- WS wrong side row

1 x 65 g *Caspian (J)
1 x 70 g *Aquamarine (K)
1 x 75 g **Peacock (H)

*Yarn colours for shawl and border
**Yarn colour for shawl and piping cord
The amount of yarn required for the border, the piping cord and the tassels/pom-poms is included in the above.

Arrangement of colours
Version 1

Each PC is being knitted for a total of 8 rows/rounds. The colour gradient scheme for PC starts with Iced (K) and ends with Cornflower (K). After the first cycle, the colour gradient scheme is reversed for the second cycle, i.e., you start out with Sky (G) - basically it is a "back and forth" rule. This way a very harmonious colour gradient is created, completely without any stripes.

Version 2

Both PC and BC respectively are knitted for a total of 5 rows/rounds each. The colour gradient scheme for PC starts with Tangerine (J) and ends with Apricot (J). The colour gradient scheme for BC starts with Kingfisher (K) and ends with Peacock (H). In total, the colour gradient schemes are repeated 3 times.

Needles

3.25 mm circular needles (with different cable lengths); adjust needle size to obtain gauge if necessary.
DPNs might be useful at the beginning of the shawl.
Knitting the border: 3 sets of 3.25 mm circular needles with 100 cm cables; adjust needle size to obtain gauge if necessary.
Knitting the piping cord of Version 2: 3 sets of 3.0 mm circular needles with 100 cm cables; adjust needle size to obtain gauge if necessary (0.25 mm smaller than the needles you used for knitting the shawl body).

Gauge

27 sts and 32 rows with 3.25 mm needles = 10 x 10 cm

Dimensions

Width 230 cm
Height 108 cm

Stitches

Stockinette stitch; two-colour Fair Isle knitting

Starting the shawl

R 1 cast-on row: co 3 sts with BC [|]
R 2 (WS): p 3 + chain cast-on 1 st [A]
R 3 (RS): k [o], k 3 sts = 4 sts, chain cast-on 1 st [A]
R 4 (WS): k [o], p 4 sts = 5 sts, chain cast-on 1 st [A]
R 5 (RS): This row marks the beginning/starting point of the patterned section. From this row onwards 1 st is increased each at the beginning [A] and at the end [+].
K R 6 (WS) up to and including R 23 (RS).

TIP: In row 20, new repeats begin on the left and right central repeat. Mark these with SMs.

Integration of steek stitches

R 23 (RS/43 sts on needle): At the end of this row chain cast-on 15 steek sts, alternating between BC and PC. Close the row to a round. From now on all sts are k sts. Continue knitting either with DPNs or using the Magic Loop technique.
Please change to Chart 2 / R 24.

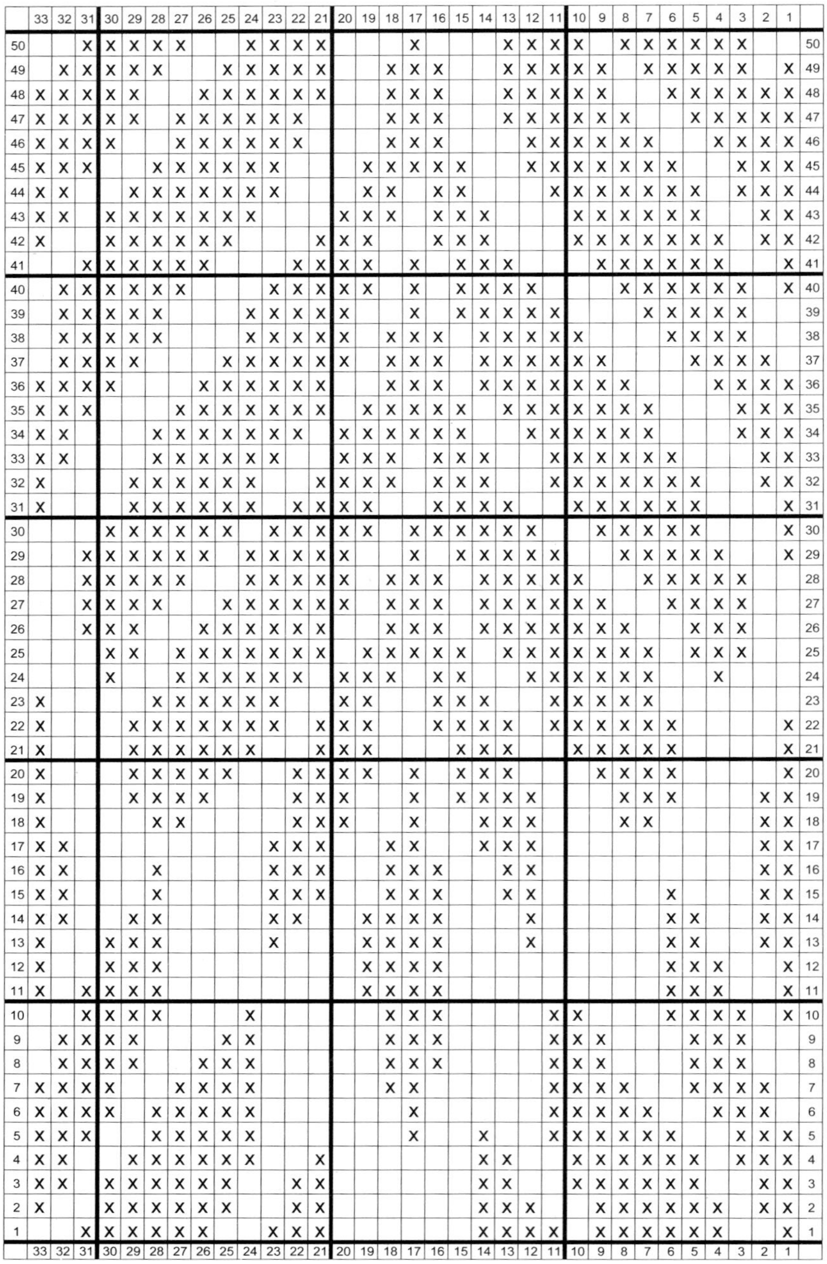

Chart 2

| | 33 | 32 | 31 | 30 | 29 | 28 | 27 | 26 | 25 | 24 | 23 | 22 | 21 | 20 | 19 | 18 | 17 | 16 | 15 | 14 | 13 | 12 | 11 | 10 | 9 | 8 | 7 | 6 | 5 | 4 | 3 | 2 | 1 | |

(Chart 2: a 50-row × 33-stitch colourwork chart with a 14/15-stitch steek section, marked with X symbols. Row numbers run 1–50 up both sides; stitch numbers 33–1 across top and bottom.)

First round with steek stitches

Start knitting R 24 with the following partition (Chart 2):

» K the last 5 sts of the repeat (from st 29 up to and including st 33).
» Move SM.
» K the 33 sts of the central repeat.
» Move SM.
» K the first 5 sts of the repeat.
» Move SM to the right needle.
» K 14 steek sts according to the established colour scheme.
» Place SM.
» K the 15th steek st.

This first round with steek stitches does not feature any increase.

All following rounds

» K all sts according to Chart 2/R 25.
» At the end of this R, inc 1 st by kfb from the last st.
» Move SM to the right needle.
» K 14 steek sts.
» Move SM to the right needle.
» Inc 1 st by kfb from the 15th steek stitch

As increases are regularly added, the pattern must also be extended to the right and left.

For better orientation, completed horizontal pattern repeats should be identified by the placement of SMs.

Once the first pattern repeat has been achieved hight-wise, start again with R 1.

In the end the shawl will be 300 rounds high (6 x 50 R of the complete pattern repeat) and 594 sts wide.
The pattern is repeated 17 times horizontally in total (17 x 33 sts = 561 sts) plus the first 16 sts of a pattern repeat on the upper left tip plus the last 16 sts of a pattern repeat on the upper right tip. Total = 594 sts.

Cutting the steek

Bind off steek sts 2 until 14 inclusive. Moisten and block the steek. When dry, secure the steek and cut it open.

Border

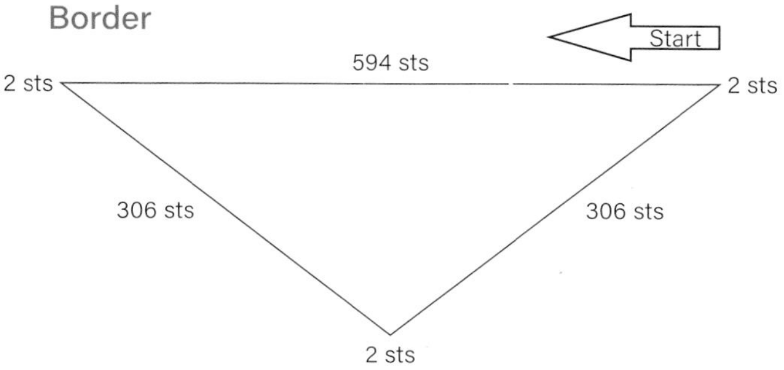

Chart3

Version 1
BC = Atlantic Spray (Re)
PC = see Chart 4

Version 2
BC = see Chart 4
PC = see Chart 4
Piping cord colour =
Peacock (H)

Version 1

K all 594 sts of the upper edge with Cornflower (K).

Inc 1 st by kfb from the 1st steek st and place SM (left tip; 2-st-marker).
Pick up and knit 306 sts on the left side.
At the bottom tip inc 2 sts and place SM (2-st-marker).
Pick up and knit 306 sts on the right side.

Inc 1 st by kfb from the 15th steek st and place SM (right tip; 2-st-marker).

Purl one round with Cornflower (K) (eyecatcher line).
At each of the 2-st-markers inc 1 st on both sides by M1R and M1L.

Each round will thus feature an increase of 6 sts.

Piping cord for Version 2

R 1: K all 594 sts of the upper edge with Peacock (H) with 3.0 mm needles; adjust needle size to obtain gauge if necessary (0.25 mm smaller than the needles you used for knitting the shawl body).

Inc 1 st by kfb from the 1st steek st and place SM (left tip; 2-st-marker).

Pick up and knit 306 sts on the left side.
At the bottom tip inc 2 sts and place SM (2-st-marker).
Pick up and knit 306 sts on the right side.

Inc 1 st by kfb from the 15th steek st and place SM (right tip; 2-st-marker).

R 2-4: K with Peacock (H) only. These rounds do not feature any increases at all.

Forming the piping cord

R 5: K with Peacock (H) and knit each and every stitch together with the corresponding stitch of R 1 on the reverse side of the border. This round does not feature any increases.

Knitting the border pattern (see p. 114)

At each of the 2-st-markers inc 1 st on both sides by M1R and M1L.

The sts of the 2-st-markers are always knitted with BC.

Please be reminded to regularly increase (2-st-markers) at all three tips of the shawl.

Due to the continuous increases, the pattern must also be extended to the left and the right.

Version 1 and Version 2 (needle size as used for the body of the shawl)

R 1-23: k the border pattern with BC and PC according to Chart 4.

Version 1

Rd 24: k with PC Atlantic Spray (Re) only.
Rd 25: p with PC Atlantic Spray (Re) only.
These rounds do not feature any increases.

Version 2 (piping cord)

R 24-27: k with Peacock (H) and with 3.0 mm needles; adjust needle size to obtain gauge if necessary (0.25 mm smaller than the needles you used for knitting the shawl body). These rounds do not feature any increases.

BORDER PATTERN

Chart 4 — pattern grid (columns 18–1) with colour columns:

18	17	16	15	14	13	12	11	10	9	8	7	6	5	4	3	2	1	PC [x] Version 1	#	PC [x] Version 2	BC [ ] Version 2
																		Atlantic Spray (Re)	49	Aquamarin (K)	
	x				x	x					x	x					x	Iced (K)	48	Elderberry (G)	Aquamarin (K)
	x				x	x					x	x					x	Iced (K)	47	Elderberry (G)	Aquamarin (K)
		x		x				x		x				x				Iced (K)	46	Elderberry (G)	Aquamarin (K)
		x	x					x	x				x	x				Iced (K)	45	Elderberry (G)	Aquamarin (K)
		x	x					x	x				x	x				Iced (K)	44	Raspberry (H)	Aquamarin (K)
	x			x				x				x				x		Iced (K)	43	Raspberry (H)	Aquamarin (K)
	x				x	x					x	x					x	Powder Blue (ReC)	42	Raspberry (H)	Caspian (J)
	x				x	x					x	x					x	Powder Blue (ReC)	41	Raspberry (H)	Caspian (J)
		x		x				x		x				x				Powder Blue (ReC)	40	Plum (J)	Caspian (J)
		x	x					x	x				x	x				Powder Blue (ReC)	39	Plum (J)	Caspian (J)
		x	x					x	x				x	x				Powder Blue (ReC)	38	Plum (J)	Caspian (J)
	x			x				x				x				x		Powder Blue (ReC)	37	Plum (J)	Caspian (J)
	x				x	x					x	x					x	Porcelain (ReU)	36	Plum (J)	Seabright (J)
	x				x	x					x	x					x	Porcelain (ReU)	35	Pink (H)	Seabright (J)
		x		x				x		x				x				Porcelain (ReU)	34	Pink (H)	Seabright (J)
		x	x					x	x				x	x				Porcelain (ReU)	33	Pink (H)	Seabright (J)
		x	x					x	x				x	x				Porcelain (ReU)	32	Pink (H)	Seabright (J)
	x			x				x				x				x		Porcelain (ReU)	31	Pink (H)	Seabright (J)
	x				x	x					x	x					x	Surf (J)	30	Carnation (Re)	Azure (Re)
	x				x	x					x	x					x	Surf (J)	29	Carnation (Re)	Azure (Re)
		x		x				x		x				x				Surf (J)	28	Carnation (Re)	Azure (Re)
		x	x					x	x				x	x				Surf (J)	27	Carnation (Re)	Azure (Re)
		x	x					x	x				x	x				Surf (J)	26	Carnation (Re)	Azure (Re)
F	**O**	**L**	**D**	**I**	**N**	**G**		**E**	**D**	**G**	**E**		**[PURL]**					Atlantic Spray (Re)	25	Rd#24-28:	
																		Atlantic Spray (Re)	24	Biese mit Peacock (H) str	
		x	x					x	x				x	x				Surf (J)	23	Carnation (Re)	Azure (Re)
		x	x					x	x				x	x				Surf (J)	22	Carnation (Re)	Azure (Re)
	x			x				x				x				x		Surf (J)	21	Carnation (Re)	Azure (Re)
	x				x	x					x	x					x	Surf (J)	20	Carnation (Re)	Azure (Re)
	x				x	x					x	x					x	Surf (J)	19	Carnation (Re)	Azure (Re)
	x			x				x				x				x		Surf (J)	18	Pink (H)	Seabright (J)
		x	x					x	x				x	x				Duck Egg (Re)	17	Pink (H)	Seabright (J)
		x	x					x	x				x	x				Duck Egg (Re)	16	Pink (H)	Seabright (J)
	x			x				x				x				x		Duck Egg (Re)	15	Pink (H)	Seabright (J)
	x				x	x					x	x					x	Duck Egg (Re)	14	Pink (H)	Seabright (J)
	x				x	x					x	x					x	Duck Egg (Re)	13	Plum (J)	Seabright (J)
	x			x				x				x				x		Duck Egg (Re)	12	Plum (J)	Caspian (J)
		x	x					x	x				x	x				Sky (G)	11	Plum (J)	Caspian (J)
		x	x					x	x				x	x				Sky (G)	10	Plum (J)	Caspian (J)
	x			x				x				x				x		Sky (G)	9	Plum (J)	Caspian (J)
	x				x	x					x	x					x	Sky (G)	8	Raspberry (H)	Caspian (J)
	x				x	x					x	x					x	Sky (G)	7	Raspberry (H)	Caspian (J)
	x			x				x				x				x		Sky (G)	6	Raspberry (H)	Aquamarin (K)
		x	x					x	x				x	x				Cornflower (K)	5	Raspberry (H)	Aquamarin (K)
		x	x					x	x				x	x				Cornflower (K)	4	Elderberry (G)	Aquamarin (K)
	x			x				x				x				x		Cornflower (K)	3	Elderberry (G)	Aquamarin (K)
	x				x	x					x	x					x	Cornflower (K)	2	Elderberry (G)	Aquamarin (K)
	x				x	x					x	x					x	Cornflower (K)	1	Elderberry (G)	Aquamarin (K)
18	17	16	15	14	13	12	11	10	9	8	7	6	5	4	3	2	1				

Chart 4

Forming the piping cord for the top edge of the shawl:

R 28: knit each and every stitch together with the corresponding stitch of R 1 on the reverse side of the border. This round does not feature any increases.

Reverse side of the border

Now all increases previously made at the three tips of the shawl border front (2-st markers) must be decreased.
In each R before and after the 2-st-marker 1 st each has to be decreased left-leaning (ssk) and right-leaning (k2tog) accordingly.

This way 6 sts are being decreased in each round.
Please follow the pattern repeats as created for the front side of the border.

Version 1

R 26-48: k the border pattern with PC and BC according to Chart 4.
R 49: k with Atlantic Spray (Re) only.

Version 2

R 29-51: k the border pattern with PC and BC according to Chart 4.
R 52: k with Aquamarine (K) only.

Cast-off all sts and sew them to the inside of the border. See the description of the "knit-and-sew cast-off" method (cf. pages 24-26).

Finishing the shawl

Wash and block the shawl.
After drying the shawl, you might want to prepare tassels/pom-poms and sew them to the tips of the shawl together with felt balls.

ROSANA

The name of this shawl says it all!
When I designed this pattern, a rose blossom immediately came to my mind. The pattern as such is knitted with one colour only. This colour should strongly contrast the many background colours, as the pattern features delicate lines and should stand out well.
The centre of the flower was knitted with a strong and dominant colour.

Yarn

Abbreviation	Yarn Manufacturer	Yardage/100g
G	Gardiner S08 Shetland (100% wool)	450m/100g
G1	Gardiner SS11 Soft Shetland (100% wool)	565m/100g
H	Harrisville New England Shetland (100% pure wool)	397m/100g
J	Jamieson of Shetland Shetland Spindrift (100% pure Shetland wool)	420m/100g
JU	Jamieson of Shetland Ultra (50% Shetland/50% lambswool)	776m/100g
K	Knoll Supersoft (100% PURE NEW WOOL)	576m/100g
SF	Lankava Esito worsted wool yarn (100% wool)	425m/100g
Ra	Rauma Finull PT2 (100% Norwegian wool)	350m/100g
Re	Rennie Supersoft (100% lambswool)	565m/100g
ReU	Rennie Unique Shetland (100% lambswool)	450m/100g
ReC	Rennie Supersoft Cashmere (87.5% lambswool/12.5% cashmere)	492m/100g
LT	Tines 100% wool	350m/100g

Shetland Spindrift, Supersoft (lambswool), pure new wool etc. The yardage of the different yarns varies. Further information can be found in the chapter concerning yarns and suppliers (see pp. 160-161).

Version 1 "Autumn Shades + Mocha"
Yarn kit "Rosana – Version 1" by Bärbel Salet VerstrickteKunst or:

350 g pattern colour(s) (PC)
Mocha (G)*

480 g background colour(s) (BC)
16 x 30 g Foliage (H), Topaz (H), Ember (K), Iron Rust (Re), Saffron (K), Lelantos (ReC), Spice (Re), Jaffa (Re), #760 Papaya (LT), Pumpkin (J), Hephaestus (ReC), #740 Orange (LT), Cornfield (J), Mustard (J), Mustard (H), Yellow Ochre (J)

The amount of yarn required for the border and the tassels/pom-poms is included in the above.

* Mocha (G) is being used for the tassels/pom-poms.

Version 2 "Pink-Fuchsia-Lilac + Aubergine"
Yarn kit "Rosana – Version 2" by Bärbel Salet VerstrickteKunst or:

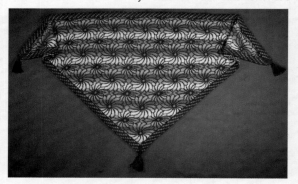

400 g pattern colour(s) (PC)
Aubergine (H)*

430 g background colour(s) (BC)
5 x 20 g Viola (K), Cottage (Re), Freesia (G), Anemone (J), Thistle (ReC)
11 x 30 g #250 Lilac (LT), Water Lily (H), #522 Flamingo (LT), Allium (K), Peony (K), Carnation (Re), Raspberry (H), Lavish (Re), Cumfrey (K), Aster (H), New Amethyst (Re)

The amount of yarn required for the border and the tassels/pom-poms is included in the above.

* Aubergine (H) is being used for the tassels/pom-poms.

Chart 1

	Version 1	Version 2
	BC = [ ]	BC = [ ]
23 (43 sts) ... RS 23	Spice (Re)	Allium (K)
22 WS (41 M) ... 22	Spice (Re)	Allium (K)
21 (39 sts) ... RS 21	Spice (Re)	Allium (K)
20 WS (37 M) ... 20	Spice (Re)	Allium (K)
19 (35 sts) ... RS 19	Lelantos (ReC)	#522 Flamingo (LT)
18 WS (33 M) ... 18	Lelantos (ReC)	#522 Flamingo (LT)
17 (31 sts) ... RS 17	Lelantos (ReC)	#522 Flamingo (LT)
16 WS (29 M) ... 16	Lelantos (ReC)	#522 Flamingo (LT)
15 (27 sts) ... RS 15	Saffron (K)	Water Lily (H)
14 WS (25 M) ... 14	Saffron (K)	Water Lily (H)
13 (23 sts) ... RS 13	Saffron (K)	Water Lily (H)
12 WS (21 M) ... 12	Iron Rust (Re)	#250 Lilac (LT)
11 (19 sts) ... RS 11	Iron Rust (Re)	#250 Lilac (LT)
10 WS (17 M) ... 10	Iron Rust (Re)	#250 Lilac (LT)
9 (15 sts) ... RS 9	Iron Rust (Re)	#250 Lilac (LT)
8 WS (13 M) ... 8	Ember (K)	Viola (K)
7 (11 sts) ... RS 7	Ember (K)	Viola (K)
6 WS (9 M) ... 6	Ember (K)	Viola (K)
5 (7 sts) ... RS 5	Ember (K)	Viola (K)
4 WS (5 M) ... 4	Ember (K)	Viola (K)
3 (4 sts) ... RS 3	Ember (K)	Viola (K)
2 WS ... 2	Ember (K)	Viola (K)
1 ... RS 1	Ember (K)	Viola (K)

Column numbers (bottom): 43 42 41 40 39 38 37 36 35 34 33 32 31 30 29 28 27 26 25 24 23 22 21 20 19 18 17 16 15 14 13 12 11 10 9 8 7 6 5 4 3 2 1

Chart1 legend

x	pattern colour(s)
(grey)	background colour(s)
I	cast-on stitches
x (dark)	pattern starting point
A	chain cast-on stitch
o	knit
+	purl bump increase
RS	right side row
WS	wrong side row

Arrangement of colours

The PC colour scheme is knitted according to a pre-determined number of rows per colour. It is important to me, that the centre of each blossom contains #760 Papaya (LT) for Version 1 and Carnation (Re) for Version 2 respectively, as these colours do form a very nice eyecatcher.

The complete colour schemes both for Version 1 and Version 2 can be found in the right-hand columns of both Chart 1 and Chart 2 respectively.

Needles

3.25 mm circular needles (with different cable lengths); adjust needle size to obtain gauge if necessary.
DPNs might be useful at the beginning of the shawl.
3 sets of 3.25 mm circular needles with 100 cm cables for knitting the border; adjust needle size to obtain gauge if necessary.

Gauge

27 sts and 32 rows with 3.25 mm needles = 10 x 10 cm

Dimensions

Width 240 cm
Height 102 cm

Stitches

Stockinette stitch; two-colour Fair Isle knitting

Starting the shawl

R 1 cast-on row: co 3 sts with BC [|]
R 2 (WS): p 3 + chain cast-on 1 st [A]
R 3 (RS): k [o], k 3 sts = 4 sts, chain cast-on 1 st [A]
R 4 (WS): k [o], p 4 sts = 5 sts, chain cast-on 1 st [A]
R 5 (RS): This row marks the beginning/starting point of the patterned section. From this row onwards 1 st is increased each at the beginning [A] and at the end [+].

K R 6 (WS) up to and including R 23 (RS) and change BC according to Chart 1.

Integration of steek stitches

R 23 (RS/43 sts on needle): At the end of this row chain cast-on 15 steek sts, alternating between BC and PC. Close the row to a round. From now on all sts are k sts. Continue knitting either with DPNs or using the Magic Loop technique.

Please change to Chart 2 / R 24.

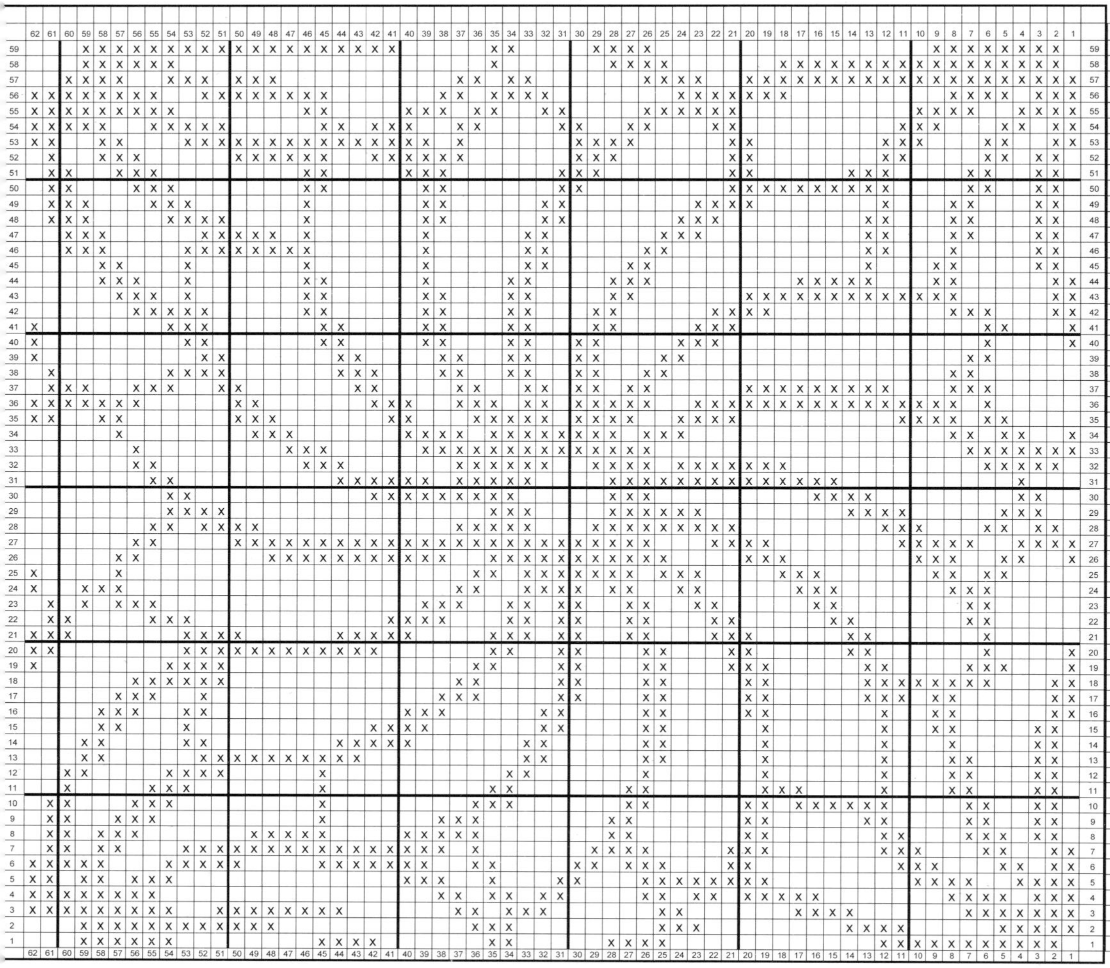

The chart on this page (Chart 2) is a colorwork knitting grid with columns numbered 62 down to 1 (left to right across the top), rows numbered 59 down to 1. Each row's "x" marks indicate stitch colours. The right-hand side lists yarn colour names per row for two versions.

Chart 2 — Colour legend (right side)

Row	Version 1 (BC = [ ])	Version 2 (BC = [ ])
59	Foliage (H)	New Amethyst (Re)
58	Foliage (H)	New Amethyst (Re)
57	Foliage (H)	New Amethyst (Re)
56	Yellow Ochre (J)	Anemone (J)
55	Yellow Ochre (J)	Anemone (J)
54	Yellow Ochre (J)	Anemone (J)
53	Mustard (H)	Fresia (G)
52	Mustard (H)	Fresia (G)
51	Mustard (H)	Fresia (G)
50	Mustard (J)	Aster (H)
49	Mustard (J)	Aster (H)
48	Mustard (J)	Aster (H)
47	Mustard (J)	Aster (H)
46	Cornfield (J)	Cottage (Re)
45	Cornfield (J)	Cottage (Re)
44	Cornfield (J)	Cottage (Re)
43	#740 Orange (LT)	Cumfrey (K)
42	#740 Orange (LT)	Cumfrey (K)
41	#740 Orange (LT)	Cumfrey (K)
40	#740 Orange (LT)	Cumfrey (K)
39	Hepha. (ReC)	Lavish (Re)
38	Hepha. (ReC)	Lavish (Re)
37	Hepha. (ReC)	Lavish (Re)
36	Pumpkin (J)	Raspberry (H)
35	Pumpkin (J)	Raspberry (H)
34	Pumpkin (J)	Raspberry (H)
33	Pumpkin (J)	Raspberry (H)
32	#760 Papaya (LT)	Carnation (Re)
31	#760 Papaya (LT)	Carnation (Re)
30	#760 Papaya (LT)	Carnation (Re)
29	#760 Papaya (LT)	Carnation (Re)
28	#760 Papaya (LT)	Carnation (Re)
27	Jaffa (Re)	Peony (K)
26	Jaffa (Re)	Peony (K)
25	Jaffa (Re)	Peony (K)
24	Jaffa (Re)	Peony (K)
23	Spice (Re)	Allium (K)
22	Spice (Re)	Allium (K)
21	Spice (Re)	Allium (K)
20	Spice (Re)	Allium (K)
19	Lelantos (ReC)	#522 Flamingo (LT)
18	Lelantos (ReC)	#522 Flamingo (LT)
17	Lelantos (ReC)	#522 Flamingo (LT)
16	Lelantos (ReC)	#522 Flamingo (LT)
15	Saffron (K)	Water Lily (H)
14	Saffron (K)	Water Lily (H)
13	Saffron (K)	Water Lily (H)
12	Iron Rust (Re)	#250 Lilac (LT)
11	Iron Rust (Re)	#250 Lilac (LT)
10	Iron Rust (Re)	#250 Lilac (LT)
9	Iron Rust (Re)	#250 Lilac (LT)
8	Ember (K)	Viola (K)
7	Ember (K)	Viola (K)
6	Ember (K)	Viola (K)
5	Topaz (H)	Thistle (ReC)
4	Topaz (H)	Thistle (ReC)
3	Topaz (H)	Thistle (ReC)
2	Foliage (H)	New Amethyst (Re)
1	Foliage (H)	New Amethyst (Re)

Chart 2

First round with steek stitches

Start knitting R 24 with the following partition (Chart 2):

» K from st 10 up to and including st 52 of the repeat.
» Place SM.
» K 14 steek sts according to the established colour scheme.
» Place SM.
» K the 15th steek st.

This first round with steek stitches does not feature any increase.

All following rounds

» K all sts according to Chart 2/R 25.
» At the end of this R, inc 1 st by kfb from the last st.
» Move SM to the right needle.
» K 14 steek sts.
» Move SM to the right needle.
» Inc 1 st by kfb from the 15th steek stitch

As increases are regularly added, the pattern must also be extended to the right and left.

For better orientation, completed horizontal pattern repeats should be identified by the placement of SMs.

Once the first pattern repeat has been achieved hight-wise, start again with R 1.

In the end the shawl will be 295 rounds high (5 x 59 R of the complete pattern repeat) and 584 sts wide.

The pattern is repeated 9 times horizontally in total (9 x 62 sts = 558 sts) plus the first 13 sts of a pattern repeat on the upper left tip and the last 13 sts of a pattern repeat on the upper right tip = 584 sts.

Cutting the steek

Bind off steek sts 2 until 14 inclusive. Moisten and block the steek. When dry, secure the steek and cut it open.

Border

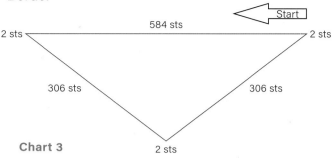

Chart 3

Version 1
BC = Mocha (G)
PC = see Chart 4

Version 2
BC = Aubergine (H)
PC = see Chart 4

K all 584 sts of the upper edge with BC.

Inc 1 st by kfb from the 1st steek st and place SM (left tip; 2-st-marker). Pick up and knit 306 sts on the left side. At the bottom tip inc 2 sts and place SM (2-st-marker). Pick up and knit 306 sts on the right side.

Inc 1 st by kfb from the 15th steek st and place SM (right tip; 2-st-marker).

Purl one round with BC (eyecatcher line).

At each of the 2-st-markers inc 1 st on both sides by M1R and M1L.

Each round will thus feature an increase of 6 sts.

BORDER PATTERN

The sts of the 2-st-markers are always knitted with BC.

	27	26	25	24	23	22	21	20	19	18	17	16	15	14	13	12	11	10	9	8	7	6	5	4	3	2	1		Version 1 PC [x]	Version 2 PC [x]
33																												33	k with BC Mocha (G) only	k with BC Aubergine (HK) only
32				x	x	x							x	x	x							x	x	x				32	Hephaestus (ReC)	Viola (K)
31				x	x	x							x	x	x							x	x	x				31	Hephaestus (ReC)	Viola (K)
30				x	x	x							x	x	x							x	x	x				30	Hephaestus (ReC)	Viola (K)
29							x	x	x							x	x	x							x	x	x	29	Pumpkin (J)	#250 Lilac (LT)
28							x	x	x							x	x	x							x	x	x	28	Pumpkin (J)	#250 Lilac (LT)
27							x	x	x							x	x	x							x	x	x	27	Pumpkin (J)	#250 Lilac (LT)
26	x	x	x							x	x	x							x	x	x							26	#760 Papaya (LT)	Water Lily (H)
25	x	x	x							x	x	x							x	x	x							25	#760 Papaya (LT)	Water Lily (H)
24	x	x	x							x	x	x							x	x	x							24	#760 Papaya (LT)	Water Lily (H)
23				x	x	x							x	x	x							x	x	x				23	Jaffa (Re)	#522 Flamingo (LT)
22				x	x	x							x	x	x							x	x	x				22	Jaffa (Re)	#522 Flamingo (LT)
21				x	x	x							x	x	x							x	x	x				21	Jaffa (Re)	#522 Flamingo (LT)
20							x	x	x							x	x	x							x	x	x	20	Spice (Re)	Allium (K)
19							x	x	x							x	x	x							x	x	x	19	Spice (Re)	Allium (K)
18							x	x	x							x	x	x							x	x	x	18	Spice (Re)	Allium (K)
17				F	O	L	D	I	N	G			E	D	G	E	[		P	U	R	L	]					17	p with BC Mocha (G) only	p with BC Aubergine (H) only
16																												16	k with BC Mocha (G) only	k with BC Aubergine (HK) only
15				x	x	x							x	x	x							x	x	x				15	Lelantos (ReC)	Cumfrey (K)
14				x	x	x							x	x	x							x	x	x				14	Lelantos (ReC)	Cumfrey (K)
13				x	x	x							x	x	x							x	x	x				13	Lelantos (ReC)	Cumfrey (K)
12	x	x	x							x	x	x							x	x	x							12	Saffron (K)	Lavish (Re)
11	x	x	x							x	x	x							x	x	x							11	Saffron (K)	Lavish (Re)
10	x	x	x							x	x	x							x	x	x							10	Saffron (K)	Lavish (Re)
9							x	x	x							x	x	x							x	x	x	9	Iron Rust (Re)	Raspberry (H)
8							x	x	x							x	x	x							x	x	x	8	Iron Rust (Re)	Raspberry (H)
7							x	x	x							x	x	x							x	x	x	7	Iron Rust (Re)	Raspberry (H)
6				x	x	x							x	x	x							x	x	x				6	Ember (K)	Carnation (Re)
5				x	x	x							x	x	x							x	x	x				5	Ember (K)	Carnation (Re)
4				x	x	x							x	x	x							x	x	x				4	Ember (K)	Carnation (Re)
3	x	x	x							x	x	x							x	x	x							3	Topaz (H)	Peony (K)
2	x	x	x							x	x	x							x	x	x							2	Topaz (H)	Peony (K)
1	x	x	x							x	x	x							x	x	x							1	Topaz (H)	Peony (K)
	27	26	25	24	23	22	21	20	19	18	17	16	15	14	13	12	11	10	9	8	7	6	5	4	3	2	1			

Chart 4

Please be reminded to regularly increase (2-st-markers) at all three tips of the shawl. Due to the continuous increases, the pattern must also be extended to the left and the right.

R 1-15: k the border pattern with BC and PC according to Chart 4.
R 16: k with BC only.
R 17: p with BC.
R 18: p with the yarn colour according to Chart 4 (folding edge).
No increases are knitted at the three tips of the shawl.

Reverse side of the border

Now all increases previously made at the three tips of the shawl border front (2-st markers) must be decreased.

In each R before and after the 2-st-marker 1 st each has to be decreased left-leaning (ssk) and right-leaning (k2tog) accordingly.

This way 6 sts are being decreased in each round.

R 18-33: k the border pattern with BC and PC according to Chart 4.

Cast-off all sts and sew them to the inside of the border. See the description of the "knit-and-sew cast-off" method (cf. pp. 24-26).

Finishing the shawl

Wash and block the shawl.
After drying the shawl, you might want to prepare tassels/ pom-poms with Mocha (G) for Version or with Aubergine (H) for Version 2 respectively, and sew them to the tips of the shawl together with felt balls.

SPIRELLI

Finding a name for this shawl was very funny. My friends and I sat
together and were pondering over possible names.
Then all of a sudden, Marlies called out, "Spirelli! ...
The pattern reminds me of the pasta!"

Yarn

Abbreviation	Yarn Manufacturer	Yardage/100g
G	Gardiner S08 Shetland (100% wool)	450m/100g
G1	Gardiner SS11 Soft Shetland (100% wool)	565m/100g
H	Harrisville New England Shetland (100% pure wool)	397m/100g
J	Jamieson of Shetland Shetland Spindrift (100% pure Shetland wool)	420m/100g
JU	Jamieson of Shetland Ultra (50% Shetland/50% lambswool)	776m/100g
K	Knoll Supersoft (100% PURE NEW WOOL)	576m/100g
SF	Lankava Esito worsted wool yarn (100% wool)	425m/100g
Ra	Rauma Finull PT2 (100% Norwegian wool)	350m/100g
Re	Rennie Supersoft (100% lambswool)	565m/100g
ReU	Rennie Unique Shetland (100% lambswool)	450m/100g
ReC	Rennie Supersoft Cashmere (87.5% lambswool/12.5% cashmere)	492m/100g
LT	Tines 100% wool	350m/100g

Shetland Spindrift, Supersoft (lambswool), pure new wool etc. The yardage of the different yarns varies. Further information can be found in the chapter concerning yarns and suppliers (see pp. 160-161).

Version 1 "Shades of Grey + Black"

Yarn kit "Spirelli – Version 1" by Bärbel Salet VerstrickteKunst or

400 g pattern colour(s) (PC)
Black (G)

420 g background colour(s) (BC)
7 x 60 g Pearl (G), Silver Grey (K), Silver Mist (H), Granite (J), Chrome (Re), Flannel Grey (K), Heron (J)

The amount of yarn required for the border is included in the above.
You might want to prepare optional tassels or pom-poms.

Version 2 " Red-Red Orange-Dark Red + Apricot"

Yarn kit "Spirelli – Version 2" by Bärbel Salet VerstrickteKunst or

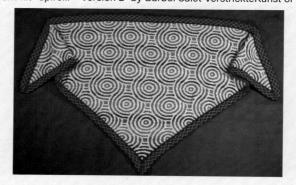

230 g pattern colour(s) (PC)
Apricot (J)

330 g background colour(s) (BC)
4 x 20 g Queen of Hearts (G), Lelantos (ReC), Brandy (K), Carmine (K)
10 x 25 g Maroon (J), Cardinal (J), Crimson (J), Red (H), Scarlet (H), #424 Red (Ra), Scarlet (Re), Poppy (H), Tudor (Re), Loganberry (G)

130 g each of Maroon (J) and Poppy (H) for the border.

The amount of yarn required for the border is included in the above.
You might want to prepare optional tassels or pom-poms.

Chart1 — Version 1

Row	Side	sts (left)	sts (right)	RS	Row	Version 1 colour
23		(43 sts)		RS	23	BC [ ]
22	WS		(41 sts)		22	Granite (J)
21		(39 sts)		RS	21	Granite (J)
20	WS		(37 sts)		20	Granite (J)
19		(35 sts)		RS	19	Granite (J)
18	WS		(33 sts)		18	Chrome (Re)
17		(31 sts)		RS	17	Chrome (Re)
16	WS		(29 sts)		16	Chrome (Re)
15		(27 sts)		RS	15	Chrome (Re)
14	WS		(25 sts)		14	Chrome (Re)
13		(23 sts)		RS	13	Chrome (Re)
12	WS		(21 sts)		12	Flannel Grey (K)
11		(19 sts)		RS	11	Flannel Grey (K)
10	WS		(17 sts)		10	Flannel Grey (K)
9		(15 sts)		RS	9	Flannel Grey (K)
8	WS		(13 sts)		8	Flannel Grey (K)
7		(11 sts)		RS	7	Flannel Grey (K)
6	WS		(9 sts)		6	Heron (J)
5		(7 sts)		RS	5	Heron (J)
4	WS		(5 sts)		4	Heron (J)
3		(4 sts)		RS	3	Heron (J)
2	WS				2	Heron (J)
1				RS	1	Heron (J)

Column numbers (bottom of chart): 43 42 41 40 39 38 37 36 35 34 33 32 31 30 29 28 27 26 25 24 23 22 21 20 19 18 17 16 15 14 13 12 11 10 9 8 7 6 5 4 3 2 1

Legend

- x pattern colour(s)
- █ background colour(s)
- ▌ cast-on stitches
- ▣ pattern starting point
- A chain cast-on stitch
- o knit
- + purl bump increase
- RS right side row
- WS wrong side row

Arrangement of colours

Version 1

Each BC is being knitted for a total of 6 rows/rounds.
The colour gradient scheme for BC starts with Heron (J) and ends with Pearl (G). After the first cycle, the colour gradient scheme is reversed for the second cycle, i.e., a total of 12 rows are knitted with Pearl (lightest grey) and Heron (darkest grey) for the transition areas – basically it is a "back and forth" rule. This way a very harmonious colour gradient is created, completely without any stripes.

Version 2

The BC gradient colour scheme is achieved with the help of previously prepared "magic balls", see the technical chapter, p. 13 ff. The wingspans are being determined individually.

Needles

3.25 mm circular needles (with different cable lengths); adjust needle size to obtain gauge if necessary.
DPNs might be useful at the beginning of the shawl.
3 sets of 3.25 mm circular needles with 100 cm cables for knitting the border; adjust needle size to obtain gauge if necessary.

Gauge

27 sts and 32 rows with 3.25 mm needles = 10 x 10 cm

Dimensions

Width 210 cm
Height 100 cm

Stitches

Stockinette stitch; two-colour Fair Isle knitting

Starting the shawl

R 1 cast-on row: co 3 sts with BC [|]
R 2 (WS): p 3 + chain cast-on 1 st [A]
R 3 (RS): k [o], k 3 sts = 4 sts, chain cast-on 1 st [A]
R 4 (WS): k [o], p 4 sts = 5 sts, chain cast-on 1 st [A]

R 5 (RS): This row marks the beginning/starting point of the patterned section. From this row onwards 1 st is increased each at the beginning [A] and at the end [+].
K R 6 (WS) up to and including R 23 (RS).

Integration of steek stitches

R 23 (RS/43 sts on needle): At the end of this row chain cast-on 15 steek sts, alternating between BC and PC. Close the row to a round. From now on all sts are k sts. Continue knitting either with DPNs or using the Magic Loop technique.

Please change to Chart 2 / R 24.

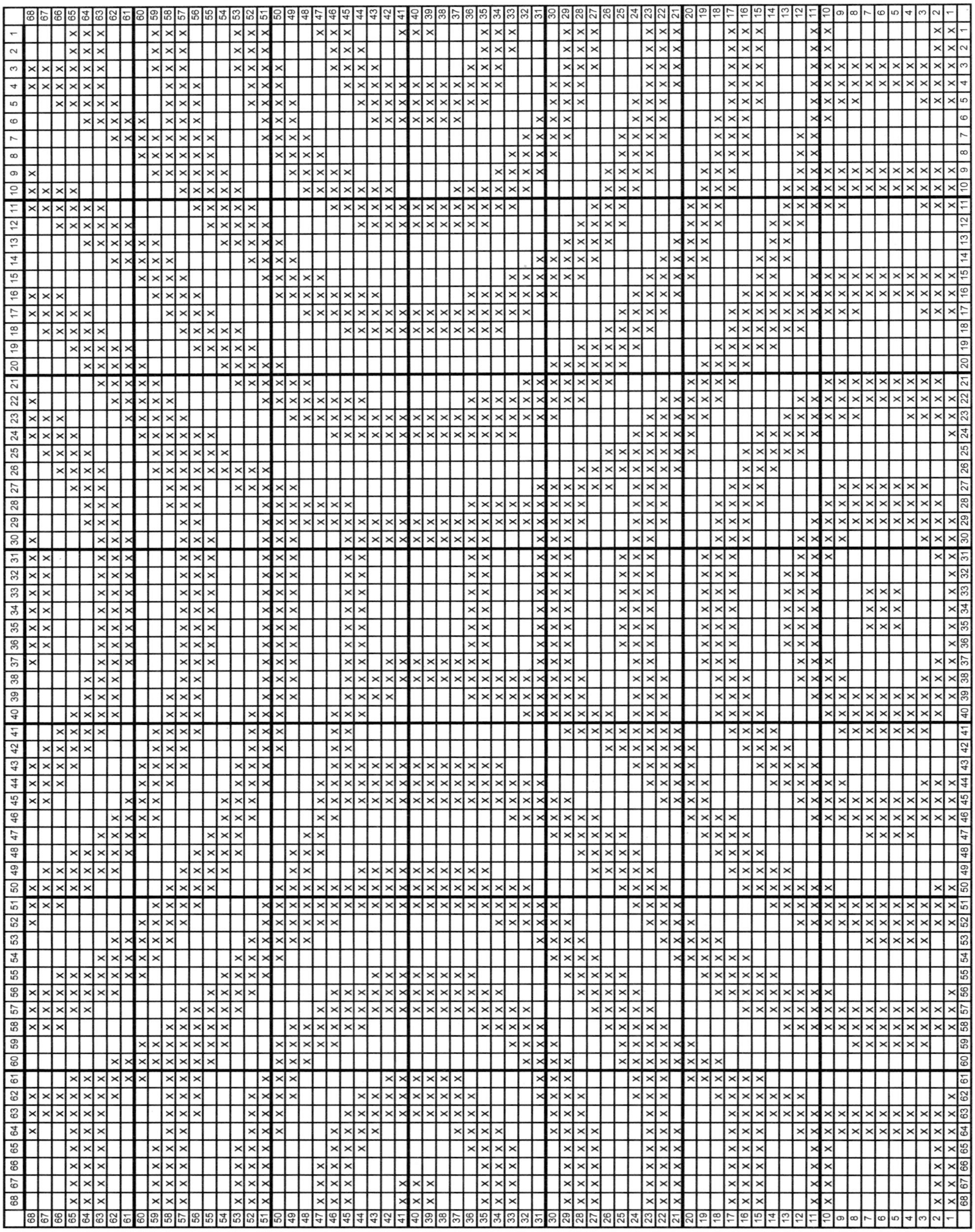

Chart 2

First round with steek stitches

Start knitting R 24 with the following partition (Chart 2):

» K from st 13 up to and including st 55.
» Place SM
» K 14 steek sts according to the established colour scheme.
» Place SM.
» K the 15th steek st.

This first round with steek stitches does not feature any increase.

From R 25 onwards and all following rounds

» K all sts according to Chart 2/R 25.
» At the end of this R, inc 1 st by kfb from the last st.
» Move SM to the right needle.
» K 14 steek sts.
» Move SM to the right needle.
» Inc 1 st by kfb from the 15th steek stitch

As increases are regularly added, the pattern must also be extended to the right and left.

For better orientation, completed horizontal pattern repeats should be identified by the placement of SMs. Once the first pattern repeat has been achieved hight-wise, start again with R 1.

In the end the shawl will be 278 rounds high (4 x 68 R of the complete pattern repeat plus one partial repeat from R 1 to and including R 6) and 550 sts wide.

The pattern is repeated 7 times horizontally in total (7 x 68 sts = 476 sts) plus the first 37 sts of a pattern repeat on the upper left tip and the last 37 sts of a pattern repeat on the upper right tip = 550 sts.

Cutting the steek

Bind off steek sts 2 until 14 inclusive. Moisten and block the steek. When dry, secure the steek and cut it open.

Border

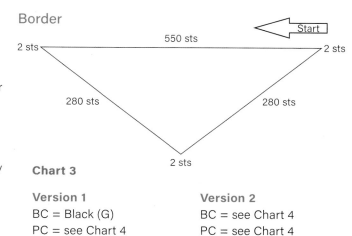

Chart 3

Version 1
BC = Black (G)
PC = see Chart 4

Version 2
BC = see Chart 4
PC = see Chart 4

K all 550 sts of the upper edge with BC Black (G) for Version 1 or Maroon (J) for Version 2.

Inc 1 st by kfb from the 1st steek st and place SM (left tip; 2-st-marker).
Pick up and knit 280 sts on the left side.
At the bottom tip inc 2 sts and place SM (2-st-marker).
Pick up and knit 280 sts on the right side.

Inc 1 st by kfb from the 15th steek st and place SM (right tip; 2-st-marker).

Purl one round with BC Black (G) for Version 1 or Maroon (J) for Version 2 (eyecatcher line).

At each of the 2-st-markers inc 1 st on both sides by M1R and M1L.

Each round will thus feature an increase of 6 sts.

BORDER PATTERN

16	15	14	13	12	11	10	9	8	7	6	5	4	3	2	1	#	PC [x]	PC [x]	PC [x]
																33	k with Black (G) only	k with Poppy (H) only	
		x	x	x							x	x	x			32	Pearl (G)	Maroon (J)	Poppy (H)
			x	x	x							x	x	x		31	Pearl (G)	Maroon (J)	Poppy (H)
	x			x	x	x				x			x	x	x	30	Pearl (G)	Maroon (J)	Poppy (H)
	x	x	x		x			x	x	x			x			29	Pearl (G)	Maroon (J)	Poppy (H)
x	x	x					x	x	x							28	Silver Grey (K)	Maroon (J)	Poppy (H)
x	x						x	x	x						x	27	Silver Grey (K)	Maroon (J)	Poppy (H)
x			x				x	x	x		x			x	x	26	Silver Grey (K)	Maroon (J)	Poppy (H)
	x	x	x			x			x		x	x	x		x	25	Silver Grey (K)	Maroon (J)	Poppy (H)
		x	x	x						x	x	x				24	Silver Mist (H)	Maroon (J)	Poppy (H)
			x	x	x						x	x	x			23	Silver Mist (H)	Maroon (J)	Poppy (H)
	x			x	x	x			x			x	x	x		22	Silver Mist (H)	Maroon (J)	Poppy (H)
	x	x	x			x		x	x	x				x		21	Silver Mist (H)	Maroon (J)	Poppy (H)
x	x	x					x	x	x							20	Granite (J)	Maroon (J)	Poppy (H)
x	x						x	x	x						x	19	Granite (J)	Maroon (J)	Poppy (H)
																18	k with Black (G) only	k with Poppy (H) only	
			FOLDING EDGE [PURL]													17	p with Black (G) only	p with Maroon (J) only	
																16	k with Black (G) only	k with Maroon (J) only	
		x	x	x							x	x	x			15	Granite (J)	Maroon (J)	Poppy (H)
			x	x	x							x	x	x		14	Granite (J)	Maroon (J)	Poppy (H)
	x			x	x	x				x			x	x	x	13	Chrome (Re)	Maroon (J)	Poppy (H)
	x	x	x		x			x	x	x			x			12	Chrome (Re)	Maroon (J)	Poppy (H)
x	x	x					x	x	x							11	Chrome (Re)	Maroon (J)	Poppy (H)
x	x						x	x	x						x	10	Chrome (Re)	Maroon (J)	Poppy (H)
x			x				x	x	x		x			x	x	9	Flannel Grey (K)	Maroon (J)	Poppy (H)
	x	x	x			x			x		x	x	x		x	8	Flannel Grey (K)	Maroon (J)	Poppy (H)
		x	x	x						x	x	x				7	Flannel Grey (K)	Maroon (J)	Poppy (H)
			x	x	x						x	x	x			6	Flannel Grey (K)	Maroon (J)	Poppy (H)
	x			x	x	x			x			x	x	x		5	Heron (J)	Maroon (J)	Poppy (H)
	x	x	x			x		x	x	x				x		4	Heron (J)	Maroon (J)	Poppy (H)
x	x	x					x	x	x							3	Heron (J)	Maroon (J)	Poppy (H)
x	x						x	x	x						x	2	Heron (J)	Maroon (J)	Poppy (H)
																1	k with Black (G) only	k with Maroon (J) only	
16	15	14	13	12	11	10	9	8	7	6	5	4	3	2	1				

Chart 4

The sts of the 2-st-markers are always knitted with BC.

The PC colour arrangement for the border [x] of Version 1 is mentioned in the right-hand side column of Chart 4. The border of Version 2 is knitted with Poppy (H) and Maroon (J), cf. Chart 4.

Please be reminded to regularly increase (2-st-markers) at all three tips of the shawl. Due to the continuous increases, the pattern must also be extended to the left and the right.

R 1: k with BC only.
R 2-15: k the border pattern with BC and PC according to Chart 4.
R 16: k with BC only.

R 17: p with BC according to Chart 4 (folding edge). No increases are knitted at the three tips of the shawl.

Reverse side of the border

Now all increases previously made at the three tips of the shawl border front (2-st markers) must be decreased.

In each R before and after the 2-st-marker 1 st each has to be decreased left-leaning (ssk) and right-leaning (k2tog) accordingly.

This way 6 sts are being decreased in each round.

Please follow the pattern repeats as created for the front side of the border.

Rd 18: k with BC only.
Rd 19-32: k the border pattern with PC and BC according to Chart 4.
Rd 33: k with BC only.

Cast-off all sts and sew them to the inside of the border.

See the description of the "knit-and-sew cast-off" method (see pp. 24-26).

Finishing the shawl

Wash and block the shawl.

After drying the shawl, you might want to prepare (optional) tassels/pom-poms and sew them to the tips of the shawl.

BOTANICO

This pattern has always reminded me of the houseplant Monstera Deliciosa. I also associate this pattern with forests, jungles, tropical rainforests or greenhouse plants in a botanical garden.

Yarn

Abbreviation	Yarn Manufacturer	Yardage/100g
G	Gardiner S08 Shetland (100% wool)	450m/100g
G1	Gardiner SS11 Soft Shetland (100% wool)	565m/100g
H	Harrisville New England Shetland (100% pure wool)	397m/100g
J	Jamieson of Shetland Shetland Spindrift (100% pure Shetland wool)	420m/100g
JU	Jamieson of Shetland Ultra (50% Shetland/50% lambswool)	776m/100g
K	Knoll Supersoft (100% PURE NEW WOOL)	576m/100g
SF	Lankava Esito worsted wool yarn (100% wool)	425m/100g
Ra	Rauma Finull PT2 (100% Norwegian wool)	350m/100g
Re	Rennie Supersoft (100% lambswool)	565m/100g
ReU	Rennie Unique Shetland (100% lambswool)	450m/100g
ReC	Rennie Supersoft Cashmere (87.5% lambswool/12.5% cashmere)	492m/100g
LT	Tines 100% wool	350m/100g

Shetland Spindrift, Supersoft (lambswool), pure new wool etc. The yardage of the different yarns varies. Further information can be found in the chapter concerning yarns and suppliers (see pp. 160-161).

Version 1 "Grey + Pink-Berry Shades"

Yarn kit "Botanico – Version 1" by Bärbel Salet VerstrickteKunst or

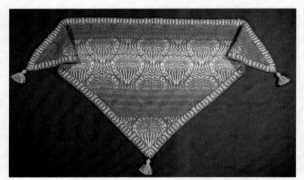

410 g pattern colour(s) (PC)

1 x 20 g Peony (K)

2 x 50 g Lavish (Re), Carnation (Re)

2 x 70 g #8014 Magenta (SF), Pink (H)

2 x 75 g Plum (J), Raspberry (H)

390 g background colour(s) (BC)

1 x 30 g Pearl (G)

6 x 50 g Silver Grey (K)*, Silver Mist (H)*, Granite (J), Chrome (Re), Flannel Grey (K)*, Dove (J)

1 x 60 g Heron (J)

The amount of yarn required for the border and the tassels is included in the above.

* Silver Grey (K)*, Silver Mist (H)* and Flannel Grey (K)* are used for the tassels.

Version 2 "Turquoise-Sea Green + Petrel"

Yarn kit "Botanico – Version 2" by Bärbel Salet VerstrickteKunst or

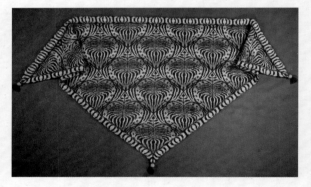

350 g pattern colour(s) (PC)

Petrel (Re)*

450g g background colour(s) (BC)

6 x 30 g Azure (Re), Seabright (J), Wood Surf (ReC), Peacock (H), Larkspur (K), Bondi Blue (Re)

6 x 45 g Mineral Blue (G), Caspian (J), Aquamarine (K), Marble Gemstone (Re), Seagreen (H), Verdigris (J)

The amount of yarn required for the border and the tassels is included in the above.

* Petrel (Re) used for the tassels.

Change BC colour	Change PC colour	Change BC colour
in every 13th row	**in every 8th row**	**in every 4th row**
R 1-13 - Pearl (G)	R 1-13 - Peony (K)	Bondi Blue (Re)
R 14 - change to Silver Grey (K)	R 14 - change to #8014 Magenta (SF)	Larkspur (K)
R 27 - change to Silver Mist (H)	R 22 - change to Carnation (Re)	Peacock (H)
R 40 - change to Granite (J)	R 30 - change to Pink (H)	Wood Surf (ReC)
R 53 - change to Chrome (Re)	R 38 - change to Plum (J)	Verdigris (J)
R 66 - change to Flannel Grey (K)	R 46 - change to Raspberry (H)	Seagreen (H)
R 79 - change to Dove (J)	R 54 - change to Lavish (Re)	Marble Gemstone (Re)
R 92 - change to Heron (J)	R 62 - change to Raspberry (H)	Aquamarine (K)
R 9 - change to Dove (J)	R 70 - change to Plum (J)	Caspian (J)
R 22 - change to Flannel Grey (K)	R 78 - change to Pink (H)	Mineral Blue (G)
R 35 - change to Chrome (Re)	R 86 - change to Carnation (Re)	Seabright (J)
R 48 - change to Granite (J)	R 94 - change to #8014 Magenta (SF)	Azure (Re)
R 61 - change to Silver Mist (H)	R 6 - change to Peony (K)	
R 74 - change to Silver Grey (K)	R 14 - change to #8014 Magenta (SF)	
R 87 - change to Pearl (G)	R 22 - change to Carnation (Re)	
R 4 - change to Silver Grey (K)	R 30 - change to Pink (H)	
R 17 - change to Silver Mist (H)	R 38 - change to Plum (J)	
R 30 - change to Granite (J)	R 46 - change to Raspberry (H)	
R 43 - change to Chrome (Re)	R 54 - change to Lavish (Re)	
R 56 - change to Flannel Grey (K)	R 62 - change to Raspberry (H)	
R 69 - change to Dove (J)	R 70 - change to Plum (J)	
R 82-96 - change to Heron (J)	R 78 - change to Pink (H)	
	R 86 - change to Carnation (Re)	
	R 94 - change to #8014 Magenta (SF)	
	R 6 - change to Peony (K)	
	R 14 - change to #8014 Magenta (SF)	
	R 22 - change to Carnation (Re)	
	R 30 - change to Pink (H)	
	R 38 - change to Plum (J)	
	R 46 - change to Raspberry (H)	
	R 54 - change to Lavish (Re)	
	R 62 - change to Raspberry (H)	
	R 70 - change to Plum (J)	
	R 78 - change to Pink (H)	
	R 86 - change to Carnation (Re)	
	R 94 - change to #8014 Magenta (SF)	

Chart 1 – Version 1

Chart 1.1 – Version 2

Arrangement of colours

Version 1

Each BC is being knitted for a total of 13 rows/rounds. The colour gradient scheme for BC starts with Pearl (G) and ends with Heron (J). After the first cycle, the colour gradient scheme is reversed for the second cycle, i.e., you continue to knit with Dove (J) – basically it is a "back and forth" rule. This way a very harmonious colour gradient is created, completely without any stripes. The PCs are changed after 8 rows/rounds each, starting with Peony (K) and ending with Lavish (Re). The second cycle is again knitted in the "back and forth" colour scheme, see Chart 1.

Version 2

The BCs are being changed after 4 rows/rounds. The colour sequence can be seen gathered from Chart 1.1. The BC gradient scheme starts with Bondi Blue (Re) and ends with Azure (Re). The background colour scheme is continuously repeated.

Needles

3.25 mm circular needles (with different cable lengths); adjust needle size to obtain gauge if necessary.
DPNs might be useful at the beginning of the shawl.
3 sets of 3.25 mm circular needles with 100 cm cables for knitting the border; adjust needle size to obtain gauge if necessary.

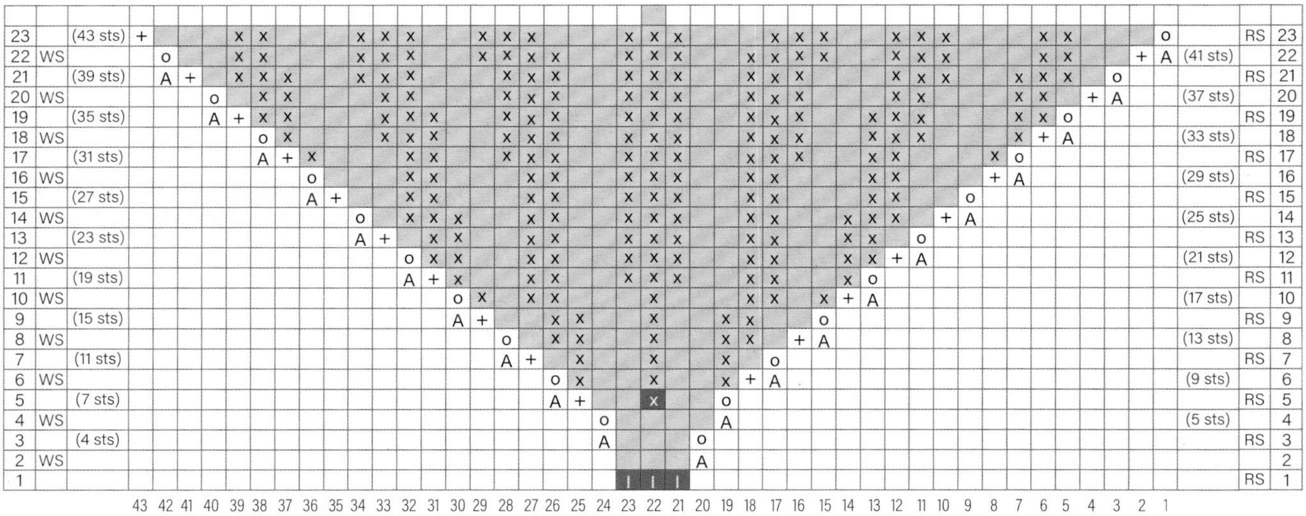

Chart 2 — Fair Isle knitting chart

Row labels (left edge → right edge):

Row	Side	Left note	Right note	Row
23	RS	(43 sts) + ... x x ... x x x ... x x x ... x x x ... x x x ... x x x ... x x ... o	RS	23
22	WS	o ... x x ... x x x ... x x x x ... x x x ... x x x x ... x x x ... x x ... + A (41 sts)		22
21	RS	(39 sts) A + x x x x ... x x x ... x x x ... x x x ... x x x ... x x x ... x x x ... o	RS	21
20	WS	o x x ... x x x ... x x x ... x x x ... x x x ... x x ... + A (37 sts)		20
19	RS	(35 sts) A + x x ... x x x ... x x x ... x x x ... x x x ... x x x ... x x o	RS	19
18	WS	o x ... x x x ... x x x ... x x x ... x x x ... x x x ... x + A (33 sts)		18
17	RS	(31 sts) A + x ... x x ... x x x ... x x x ... x x x ... x x ... x o	RS	17
16	WS	o ... x x ... x x x ... x x x ... x x ... x x ... + A (29 sts)		16
15	RS	(27 sts) A + ... x x ... x x x ... x x x ... x x ... x x ... o	RS	15
14	WS	o ... x x x ... x x ... x x x ... x x ... x x x ... + A (25 sts)		14
13	RS	(23 sts) A + ... x x ... x x x ... x x x ... x x ... x x ... o	RS	13
12	WS	o x x ... x x ... x x x ... x x ... x x ... + A (21 sts)		12
11	RS	(19 sts) A + x ... x x ... x x x ... x x ... x o	RS	11
10	WS	o x ... x x ... x ... x x ... x + A (17 sts)		10
9	RS	(15 sts) A + ... x x ... x ... x x ... o	RS	9
8	WS	o ... x x ... x ... x x ... + A (13 sts)		8
7	RS	(11 sts) A + ... x ... x ... x ... o	RS	7
6	WS	o x ... x ... x + A (9 sts)		6
5	RS	(7 sts) A + x o	RS	5
4	WS	o ... A (5 sts)		4
3	RS	(4 sts) A ... o	RS	3
2	WS	A		2
1	RS				RS	1

Column numbers (right to left): 43 42 41 40 39 38 37 36 35 34 33 32 31 30 29 28 27 26 25 24 23 22 21 20 19 18 17 16 15 14 13 12 11 10 9 8 7 6 5 4 3 2 1

Chart 2 legend:

x	pattern colour(s)	I	cast-on stitches	A	chain cast-on stitch	RS	right side row
(shaded)	background colour(s)	x (dark)	pattern starting point	o	knit	WS	wrong side row
				+	purl bump increase		

Gauge

27 sts and 32 rows with 3.25 mm needles = 10 x 10 cm

Dimensions

Width 210 cm
Height 96 cm

Stitches

Stockinette stitch; two-colour Fair Isle knitting

Starting the shawl

R 1 cast-on row: co 3 sts with BC [|]
R 2 (WS): p 3 + chain cast-on 1 st [A]
R 3 (RS): k [o], k 3 sts = 4 sts, chain cast-on 1 st [A]
R 4 (WS): k [o], p 4 sts = 5 sts, chain cast-on 1 st [A]
R 5 (RS): This row marks the beginning/starting point of the patterned section. From this row onwards 1 st is increased each at the beginning [A] and at the end [+].
K R 6 (WS) up to and including R 23 (RS).

Integration of steek stitches

R 23 (RS/43 sts on needle): At the end of this row chain cast-on 15 steek sts, alternating between BC and PC. Close the row to a round. From now on all sts are k sts. Continue knitting either with DPNs or using the Magic Loop technique.
Please change to Chart 3 / R 24.

First round with steek stitches

Start knitting R 24 with the following partition (Chart 2):
» K from st 30 up to and including st 72.
» Place SM.
» K 14 steek sts according to the established colour scheme.
» Place SM.
» K the 15th steek st.

This first round with steek stitches does not feature any increase.

From R 25 onwards and all following rounds

» K all sts according to Chart 3/R 25.
» At the end of this R, inc 1 st by kfb from the last st.
» Move SM to the right needle.
» K 14 steek sts.
» Move SM to the right needle.
» Inc 1 st by kfb from the 15th steek stitch

As increases are regularly added, the pattern must also be extended to the right and left.

For better orientation, completed horizontal pattern repeats should be identified by the placement of SMs. Once the first pattern repeat has been achieved hightwise, start again with R 1.

In the end the shawl will be 288 rounds high (3 x 96 R of the complete pattern repeat) and 570 sts wide.

Chart 3

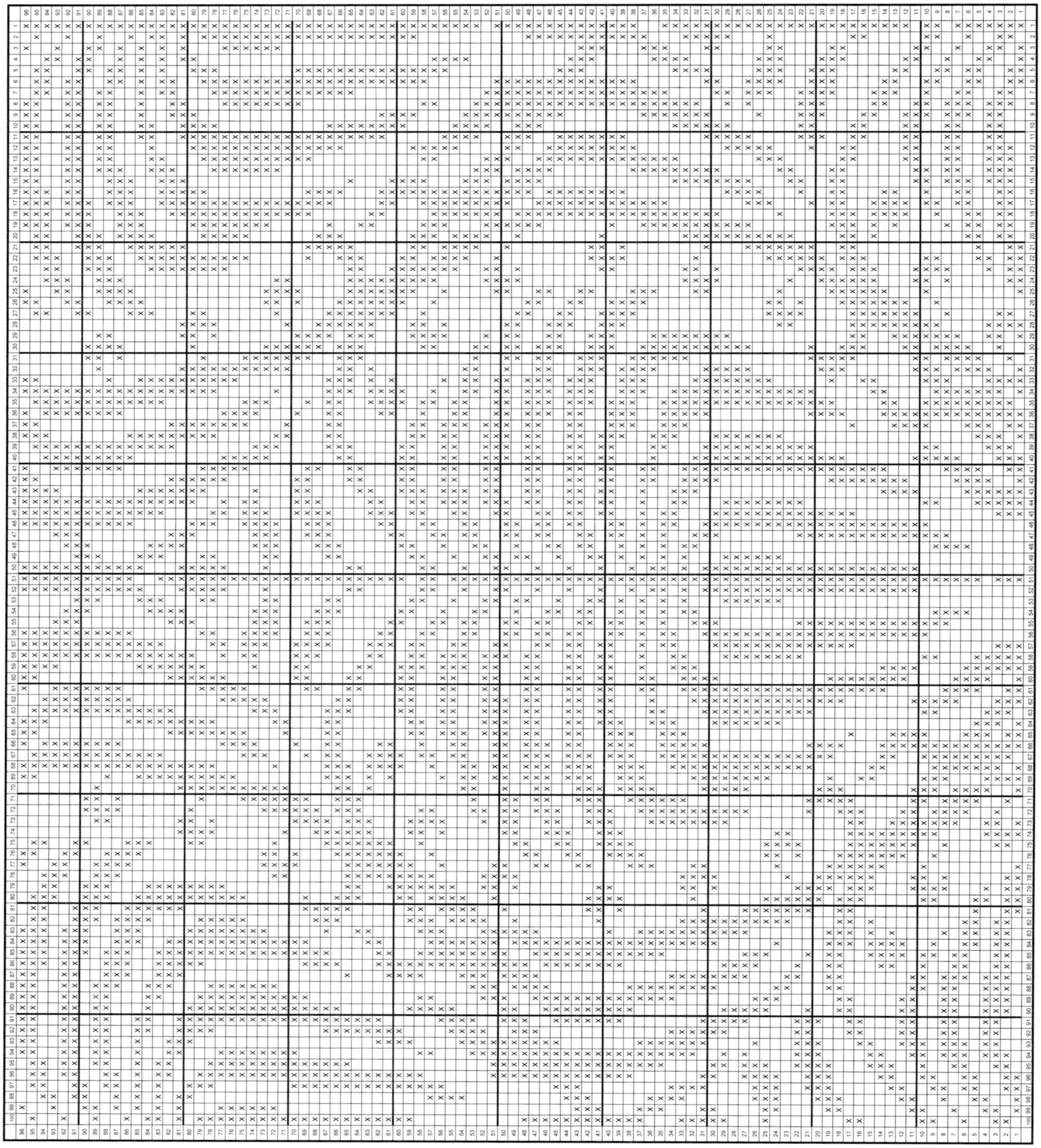

140

The pattern is repeated 5 times horizontally in total (5 x 100 sts = 500 sts) plus the first 35 sts of a pattern repeat on the upper left tip and the last 35 sts of a pattern repeat on the upper right tip = 570 sts.

Cutting the steek

Bind off steek sts 2 until 14 inclusive. Moisten and block the steek. When dry, secure the steek and cut it open.

Border

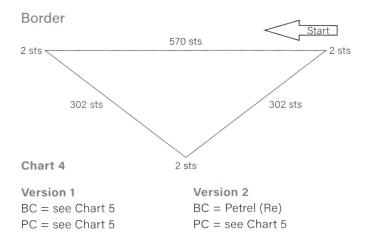

Chart 4

Version 1
BC = see Chart 5
PC = see Chart 5

Version 2
BC = Petrel (Re)
PC = see Chart 5

K all 570 sts of the upper edge with #8014 Magenta (SF) for Version 1 or Petrel (Re) for Version 2.

Inc 1 st by kfb from the 1st steek st and place SM (left tip; 2-st-marker).
Pick up and knit 302 sts on the left side.
At the bottom tip inc 2 sts and place SM (2-st-marker).
Pick up and knit 302 sts on the right side.

Inc 1 st by kfb from the 15th steek st and place SM (right tip; 2-st-marker).

Purl one round with #8014 Magenta (SF) for Version 1 or Petrel (Re) for Version 2 (eyecatcher line).

At each of the 2-st-markers inc 1 st on both sides by M1R and M1L.

Each round will thus feature an increase of 6 sts.

BORDER PATTERN

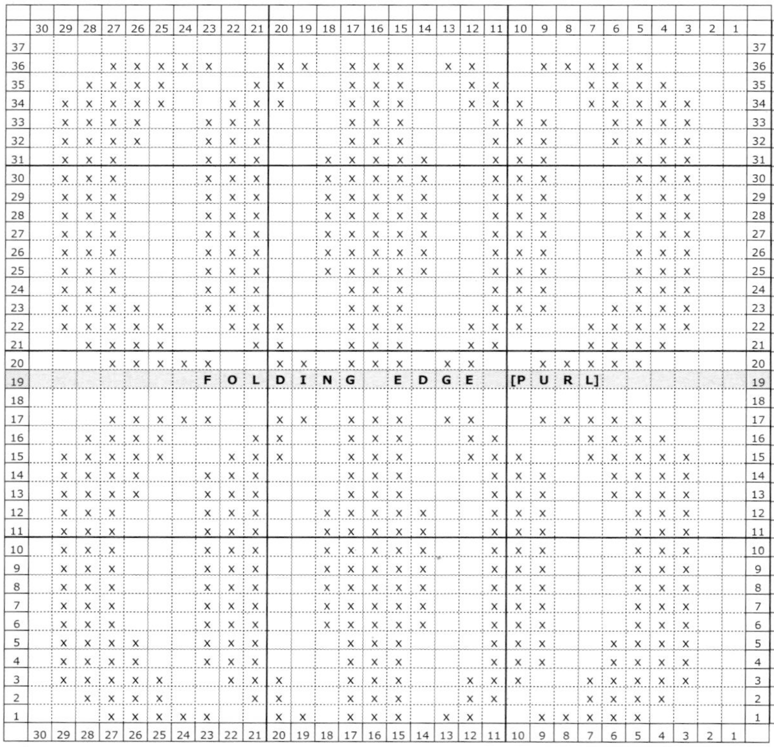

Chart 5

The following color legend corresponds to Chart 5:

	Version 1		Version 2	
Row	PC [x]	BC [ ]	PC [x]	BC [ ]
37	Heron (J)		Petrel (Re)	
36	Lavish (Re)	Heron (J)	Verdigris (J)	Petrel
35	Lavish (Re)	Heron (J)	Verdigris (J)	Petrel
34	Lavish (Re)	Heron (J)	Verdigris (J)	Petrel
33	Lavish (Re)	Heron (J)	Seagreen (H)	Petrel
32	Lavish (Re)	Heron (J)	Seagreen (H)	Petrel
31	Lavish (Re)	Heron (J)	Seagreen (H)	Petrel
30	Lavish (Re)	Dove (J)	Mar. Gemstone (Re)	Petrel
29	Lavish (Re)	Dove (J)	Mar. Gemstone (Re)	Petrel
28	Raspberry (H)	Dove (J)	Mar. Gemstone (Re)	Petrel
27	Raspberry (H)	Dove (J)	Aquamarine (K)	Petrel
26	Raspberry (H)	Dove (J)	Aquamarine (K)	Petrel
25	Raspberry (H)	Flannel Grey (K)	Aquamarine (K)	Petrel
24	Raspberry (H)	Flannel Grey (K)	Caspian (J)	Petrel
23	Raspberry (H)	Flannel Grey (K)	Caspian (J)	Petrel
22	Plum (J)	Flannel Grey (K)	Caspian (J)	Petrel
21	Plum (J)	Flannel Grey (K)	Mineral Blue (G)	Petrel
20	Plum (J)	Chrom (Re)	Mineral Blue (G)	
19	Plum (J)		Petrel	
18	Plum (J)		Petrel	
17	Plum (J)	Chrom (Re)	Mineral Blue (G)	Petrel
16	Plum (J)	Chrom (Re)	Mineral Blue (G)	Petrel
15	Plum (J)	Chrom (Re)	Caspian (J)	Petrel
14	Pink (H)	Granite (J)	Caspian (J)	Petrel
13	Pink (H)	Granite (J)	Caspian (J)	Petrel
12	Pink (H)	Granite (J)	Aquamarine (K)	Petrel
11	Pink (H)	Silver Mist (H)	Aquamarine (K)	Petrel
10	Carnation (Re)	Silver Mist (H)	Aquamarine (K)	Petrel
9	Carnation (Re)	Silver Mist (H)	Mar. Gemstone (Re)	Petrel
8	Carnation (Re)	Silver Mist (H)	Mar. Gemstone (Re)	Petrel
7	Carnation (Re)	Silver Grey (K)	Mar. Gemstone (Re)	Petrel
6	#8014 Magenta (SF)	Silver Grey (K)	Seagreen (H)	Petrel
5	#8014 Magenta (SF)	Silver Grey (K)	Seagreen (H)	Petrel
4	#8014 Magenta (SF)	Silver Grey (K)	Seagreen (H)	Petrel
3	#8014 Magenta (SF)	Silver Grey (K)	Verdigris (J)	Petrel
2	#8014 Magenta (SF)	Silver Grey (K)	Verdigris (J)	Petrel
1	#8014 Magenta (SF)	Silver Grey (K)	Verdigris (J)	Petrel

Row 19 of the chart reads: **FOLDING EDGE [PURL]**

The sts of the 2-st-markers are always knitted with BC.

Please be reminded to regularly increase (2-st-markers) at all three tips of the shawl. Due to the continuous increases, the pattern must also be extended to the left and the right.

R 1-17: k the border pattern with BC and PC according to Chart 5.
R 18: k with the yarn colour in Chart 5 only.
R 19: p with the yarn colour according to Chart 5 (folding edge).

No increases are knitted at the three tips of the shawl.

Reverse side of the border

Now all increases previously made at the three tips of the shawl border front (2-st markers) must be decreased.

In each R before and after the 2-st-marker 1 st each has to be decreased left-leaning (ssk) and right-leaning (k2tog) accordingly.

This way 6 sts are being decreased in each round.

Please follow the pattern repeats as created for the front side of the border.

R 20-36: k the border pattern with BC and PC according to Chart 5.
R 37: k with the yarn colour according to Chart 5.

Cast-off all sts and sew them to the inside of the border. See the description of the "knit-and-sew cast-off" method (see pp. 24-26).

Finishing the shawl

Wash and block the shawl.
After drying the shawl, you might want to prepare tassels and sew them to the tips of the shawl together with felt balls.

BIGGI

What do a bicycle breakdown and an old embroidery design have in common?

Many years ago, I discovered a very old book of embroidery designs among my late mother-in-law's belongings. A flower pattern contained therein was my inspiration for the present design. After many colour tests, I was not convinced whether it could be used or not and archived the pattern.

Biggi lives in New Zealand and we have been following each other's Instagram accounts for quite some time, when she reported a bicycle breakdown and posted photos of the flat tyre and of her outfit. I was quite excited to see the colours of her ©Cycology cycling jacket. Colourful flowers in my favourite colours of orange, pink, red-orange were combined with a dark burgundy shade. Beautiful! This play of colours! And it suddenly "clicked"!

Yarn

Abbreviation	Yarn Manufacturer	Yardage/100g
G	Gardiner S08 Shetland (100% wool)	450 m/100g
G1	Gardiner SS11 Soft Shetland (100% wool)	565 m/100g
H	Harrisville New England Shetland (100% pure wool)	397m/100g
J	Jamieson of Shetland Shetland Spindrift (100% pure Shetland wool)	420 m/100g
JU	Jamieson of Shetland Ultra (50% Shetland/50% lambswool)	776m/100g
K	Knoll Supersoft (100% PURE NEW WOOL)	576m/100g
SF	Lankava Esito worsted wool yarn (100% wool)	425 m/100g
Ra	Rauma Finull PT2 (100% Norwegian wool)	350 m/100g
Re	Rennie Supersoft (100% lambswool)	565 m/100g
ReU	Rennie Unique Shetland (100% lambswool)	450 m/100g
ReC	Rennie Supersoft Cashmere (87.5% lambswool/ 12.5% cashmere)	492 m/100g
LT	Tines 100% wool	350 m/100g

Shetland Spindrift, Supersoft (lambswool), pure new wool etc. The yardage of the different yarns varies. Further information can be found in the chapter concerning yarns and suppliers (see pp. 160-161).

Version 1 "Pink-Orange-Red Orange + Port Wine"

Yarn kit "Biggi – Version 1" by Bärbel Salet VerstrickteKunst or

455 g pattern colour(s) (PC)

11 x 20 g Scarlet (Re), Spice (Re), Sunset (G1), Jaffa (Re), Fuchsia (J), Sherbet (J), Peony (K), Carnation (Re), Pink (H), Poppy (K), #424 Red (Ra)
7 x 25 g Pumpkin (J), #760 Papaya (LT), Zinnia (H), #4886 Dark Cherry (Ra), Plum (J), Scarlet (J), Coral (ReU), Zinnia (H)
2 x 30 g Poppy (H), Raspberry (H)

440 g background colour(s) (BC)

Port Wine (J)

Piping cord and tassels: 45 g New Lawn (Re), 65 g Calypso (Re) The amount of yarn required for the border is included in the above.

Version 2 "Yellow-Light Green-Natural + Pine"

Yarn kit "Biggi – Version 2" by Bärbel Salet VerstrickteKunst or

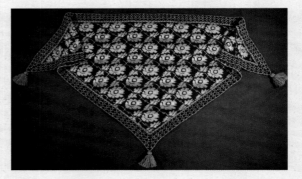

455 g pattern colour(s) (PC)

5 x 15 g Stonehenge (Re), Spring Meadow (Re), #8036 Light green (SF), Verbena (K), Chartreuse (J)
7 x 20 g Straw (H), Goldenrod (H), #8037 Pistachio green (SF), Lime Sorbet (ReC), Pistachio (J), Tundra (H), Gold (J)
2 x 30 g Pistachio (Re)*, Almond (K)
2 x 40 g Laurel (ReU), Bleached White (K),
2 x 50 g Marigold (H)*, Mimosa (J)*

440 g background colour(s) (BC)

Pine (J)

Piping cord and tassels: 45 g Azure (Re), 65 g Marble Gemstone (Re)

The amount of yarn required for the border (PCs = Marigold (H), Pistachio (Re), Mimosa (J)) is included in the above.

Arrangement of colours

The PC colour scheme is knitted according to a certain sequence of rows per colour. These can be found in the right-hand columns of both Chart 1 and Chart 2 respectively.

Needles

3.25 mm circular needles (with different cable lengths); adjust needle size to obtain gauge if necessary.
DPNs might be useful at the beginning of the shawl. 3 sets of 3.25 mm circular needles with 100 cm cables for knitting the border; adjust needle size to obtain gauge if necessary.

Gauge

27 sts and 32 rows with 3.25 mm needles = 10 x 10 cm

Dimensions

Width 253 cm
Height 109 cm

Stitches

Stockinette stitch; two-colour Fair Isle knitting

Starting the shawl

R 1 cast-on row: co 3 sts with BC [|]
R 2 (WS): p 3 + chain cast-on 1 st [A]
R 3 (RS): k [o], k 3 sts = 4 sts, chain cast-on 1 st [A]
R 4 (WS): k [o], p 4 sts = 5 sts, chain cast-on 1 st [A]
R 5 (RS): This row marks the beginning/starting point of the patterned section. From this row onwards 1 st is increased each at the beginning [A] and at the end [+].

K R 6 (WS) up to and including R 23 (RS) according to Chart 1.

R 6 (RR) bis R 23 (HR) lt. Chart 1 stricken.

Integration of steek stitches

R 23 (RS/43 sts on needle): At the end of this row chain cast-on 15 steek sts, alternating between BC and PC. Close the row to a round. From now on all sts are k sts. Continue knitting either with DPNs or using the Magic Loop technique.

Please change to Chart 2 / R 24.

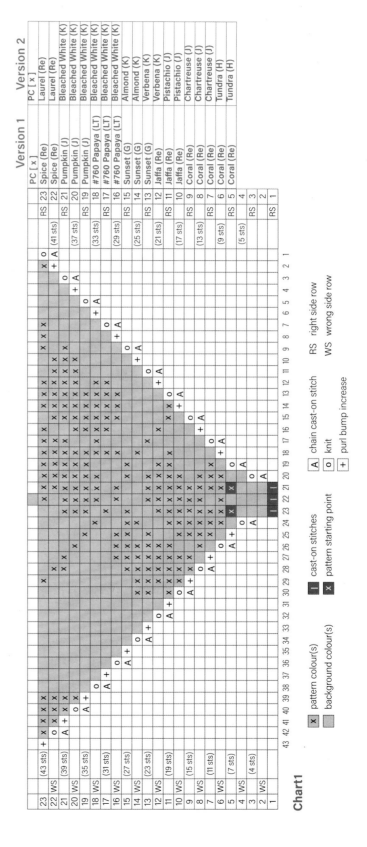

Chart 1

RS right side row
WS wrong side row

A chain cast-on stitch
A knit
o knit
+ purl bump increase

cast-on stitches
pattern starting point

pattern colour(s)
background colour(s)

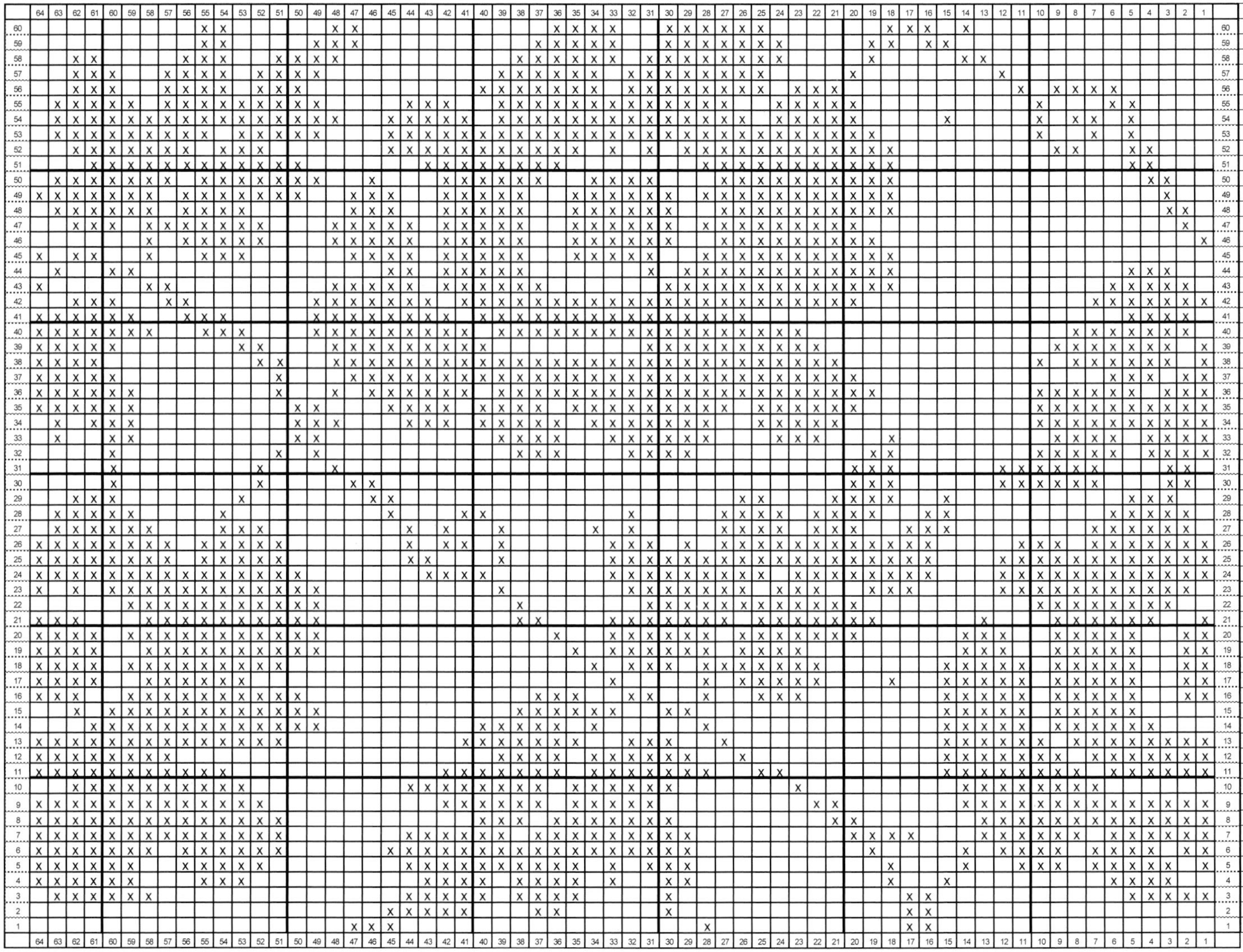

Version 2 / **Version 1**

#	Version 2	Version 1
60	Gold (J)	Sherbet (J)
59	Straw (H)	Sherbet (J)
58	Straw (H)	Sherbet (J)
57	Straw (H)	Peony (K)
56	Goldenrod (H)	Peony (K)
55	Goldenrod (H)	Peony (K)
54	Marigold (H)	Carnation (Re)
53	Marigold (H)	Carnation (Re)
52	Marigold (H)	Carnation (Re)
51	Mimosa (J)	Raspberry (H)
50	Mimosa (J)	Raspberry (H)
49	Mimosa (J)	Pink (H)
48	Mimosa (J)	Pink (H)
47	Mimosa (J)	Pink (H)
46	Mimosa (J)	#4886 Dark Cherry (Ra)
45	Pistachio (Re)	#4886 Dark Cherry (Ra)
44	Pistachio (Re)	#4886 Dark Cherry (Ra)
43	Pistachio (Re)	#4886 Dark Cherry (Ra)
42	Pistachio (Re)	Plum (J)
41	#8037 Pistazie (SF)	Plum (J)
40	#8037 Pistazie (SF)	Poppy (K)
39	#8037 Pistazie (SF)	Poppy (K)
38	Lime Sorbet (Re)	Poppy (K)
37	Lime Sorbet (Re)	Scarlet (J)
36	Lime Sorbet (Re)	Scarlet (J)
35	Lime Sorbet (Re)	Scarlet (J)
34	Stonehenge (Re)	Scarlet (J)
33	Stonehenge (Re)	#424 Red (Ra)
32	Stonehenge (Re)	#424 Red (Ra)
31	Spring Meadow (Re)	#424 Red (Ra)
30	Spring Meadow (Re)	Scarlet (Re)
29	Spring Meadow (Re)	Scarlet (Re)
28	#8036 Light green (SF)	Poppy (H)
27	#8036 Light green (SF)	Poppy (H)
26	#8036 Light green (SF)	Poppy (H)
25	Laurel (Re)	Spice (Re)
24	Laurel (Re)	Spice (Re)
23	Laurel (Re)	Spice (Re)
22	Bleached White (K)	Pumpkin (J)
21	Bleached White (K)	Pumpkin (J)
20	Bleached White (K)	Pumpkin (J)
19	Bleached White (K)	#760 Papaya (LT)
18	Bleached White (K)	#760 Papaya (LT)
17	Almond (K)	#760 Papaya (LT)
16	Almond (K)	Sunset (G)
15	Verbena (K)	Sunset (G)
14	Verbena (K)	Sunset (G)
13	Pistachio (J)	Jaffa (Re)
12	Pistachio (J)	Jaffa (Re)
11	Chartreuse (J)	Jaffa (Re)
10	Chartreuse (J)	Coral (Re)
9	Chartreuse (J)	Coral (Re)
8	Tundra (H)	Coral (Re)
7	Tundra (H)	Zinnia (H)
6	Tundra (H)	Zinnia (H)
5	Gold (J)	Zinnia (H)
4	Gold (J)	Fuchsia (J)
3	Gold (J)	Fuchsia (J)
2		Fuchsia (J)

PC [x]

Chart 2

First round with steek stitches

Start knitting R 24 with the following partition (Chart 2):

» K from st 11 up to and including st 53.
» Place SM.
» K 14 steek sts according to the established colour scheme.
» Place SM.
» K the 15th steek st.

This first round with steek stitches does not feature any increase.

All following rounds

» K all sts according to Chart 2/R 25.
» At the end of this R, inc 1 st by kfb from the last st.
» Move SM to the right needle.
» K 14 steek sts.
» Move SM to the right needle.
» Inc 1 st by kfb from the 15th steek stitch

As increases are regularly added, the pattern must also be extended to the right and left.

For better orientation, completed horizontal pattern repeats should be identified by the placement of SMs.

Once the first pattern repeat has been achieved hight-wise, start again with R 1.

In R 301 (knitted with BC only; final round):
Duplicate the 298th st by way of kfb = 597 sts.
This makes it easier to work the piping cord in a most accurate way.

In the end the shawl will be 301 rounds high (5 x 60 R of the complete pattern repeat plus one round knitted with BC only). The pattern is repeated 9 times horizontally in total (9 x 64 sts = 576 sts) plus the first 9 sts of a pattern repeat plus 1 st added in R 301 on the upper left tip (= 10 sts) and the last 9 sts of a pattern repeat plus 1 st added in R 301 on the upper right tip (= 10 sts) plus 1 st in the middle of R 301 = 597 sts.

Cutting the steek

Bind off steek sts 2 until 14 inclusive. Moisten and block the steek. When dry, secure the steek and cut it open.

Border

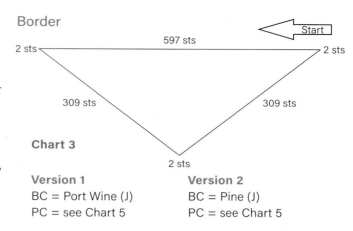

Chart 3

Version 1
BC = Port Wine (J)
PC = see Chart 5

Version 2
BC = Pine (J)
PC = see Chart 5

Piping cord colours

Version 1
light green = Calypso (Re)
dark green = New Lawn (Re)

Version 2
light turquoise = Marble Gemstone (Re)
dark turquoise = Azure (Re)

Piping cord pattern

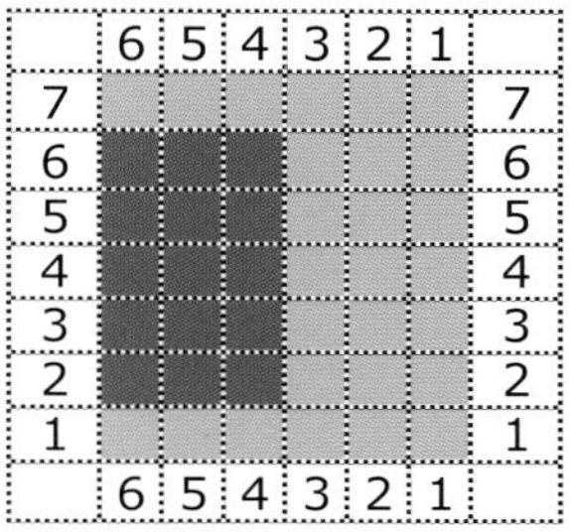

Chart 4.1 - Version 1

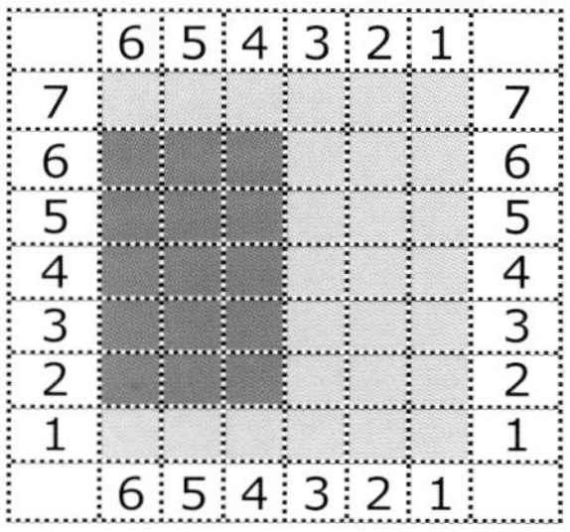

Chart 4.2 - Version 2

	32	31	30	29	28	27	26	25	24	23	22	21	20	19	18	17	16	15	14	13	12	11	10	9	8	7	6	5	4	3	2	1		Version 1 PC [x]	Version 2 PC [x]
55		x	x	x	x	x	x	x		x	x	x	x	x	x	x		x	x	x	x	x	x		x	x	x	x	x	x	x	x	55	Spice (Re)	Laurel (Re)
54		x						x		x				x		x							x		x							x	54	Spice (Re)	Laurel (Re)
53			x			x				x				x				x			x		x			x			x				53	Spice (Re)	Laurel (Re)
52			x			x				x				x				x			x		x			x			x				52	Pumpkin (J)	Laurel (Re)
51				x		x				x		x		x					x			x					x		x				51	Pumpkin (J)	Laurel (Re)
50				x		x				x				x					x			x					x		x				50	Pumpkin (J)	Laurel (Re)
49					x					x					x					x				x			x						49	#760 Papaya (LT)	Laurel (Re)
48					x					x					x					x				x			x						48	#760 Papaya (LT)	Laurel (Re)
47		x	x	x	x	x	x		x	x	x	x	x	x	x		x	x	x	x	x	x		x	x	x	x	x	x	x	x	x	47	#760 Papaya (LT)	Bleached White (K)
46		x						x		x				x		x							x		x							x	46	Sunset (G)	Bleached White (K)
45			x			x				x				x				x			x		x			x			x				45	Sunset (G)	Bleached White (K)
44			x			x				x				x				x			x		x			x			x				44	Sunset (G)	Bleached White (K)
43				x		x				x		x		x					x			x					x		x				43	Jaffa (Re)	Bleached White (K)
42				x		x				x		x		x					x			x					x		x				42	Jaffa (Re)	Bleached White (K)
41					x					x					x					x				x									41	Jaffa (Re)	Bleached White (K)
40					x					x					x					x				x									40	Coral (Re)	Bleached White (K)
39		x	x	x	x	x	x		x	x	x	x	x	x	x		x	x	x	x	x	x		x	x	x	x	x	x	x	x	x	39	Coral (Re)	Almond (K)
38		x						x		x				x		x							x		x							x	38	Coral (Re)	Almond (K)
37			x			x				x				x				x			x		x			x			x				37	Zinnia (H)	Almond (K)
36			x			x				x				x				x			x		x			x			x				36	Zinnia (H)	Almond (K)
35				x		x				x		x		x					x			x					x		x				35	Zinnia (H)	Almond (K)
34				x		x				x		x		x					x			x					x		x				34	Fuchsia (J)	Almond (K)
33					x					x					x					x				x									33	Fuchsia (J)	Almond (K)
32					x					x					x					x				x									32	Fuchsia (J)	Almond (K)
31																																	31	Chart#4.1	Chart#4.2
30																																	30	Chart#4.1	Chart#4.2
29																																	29	Chart#4.1	Chart#4.2
28							P	I	P	I	N	G		C	O	R	D																28	Chart#4.1	Chart#4.2
27																																	27	Chart#4.1	Chart#4.2
26																																	26	Chart#4.1	Chart#4.2
25																																	25	Chart#4.1	Chart#4.2
24				x						x					x					x				x									24	Sherbet (J)	Marigold (H)
23				x						x					x					x				x									23	Sherbet (J)	Marigold (H)
22				x		x				x		x		x					x			x					x		x				22	Peony (K)	Marigold (H)
21				x		x				x		x		x					x			x					x		x				21	Peony (K)	Marigold (H)
20			x			x				x				x				x			x		x			x			x				20	Carnation (Re)	Marigold (H)
19			x			x				x				x				x			x		x			x			x				19	Carnation (Re)	Marigold (H)
18		x						x		x				x		x							x		x							x	18	Raspberry (H)	Marigold (H)
17		x	x	x	x	x	x		x	x	x	x	x	x	x		x	x	x	x	x	x		x	x	x	x	x	x	x	x	x	17	Raspberry (H)	Marigold (H)
16				x		x				x				x				x			x		x			x			x				16	Pink (H)	Minosa (J)
15				x		x				x				x				x			x		x			x			x				15	Pink (H)	Minosa (J)
14				x		x				x		x		x					x			x					x		x				14	#4886 Dark Cherry (Ra)	Minosa (J)
13				x		x				x		x		x					x			x					x		x				13	#4886 Dark Cherry (Ra)	Minosa (J)
12			x			x				x				x				x			x		x			x			x				12	Plum (J)	Minosa (J)
11			x			x				x				x				x			x		x			x			x				11	Plum (J)	Minosa (J)
10		x						x		x				x		x							x		x							x	10	Poppy (K)	Minosa (J)
9		x	x	x	x	x	x		x	x	x	x	x	x	x		x	x	x	x	x	x		x	x	x	x	x	x	x	x	x	9	Poppy (K)	Minosa (J)
8				x						x					x					x				x									8	Scarlet (J)	Pistachio (Re)
7				x						x					x					x				x									7	Scarlet (J)	Pistachio (Re)
6			x			x				x		x		x					x			x					x		x				6	#424 Red (Ra)	Pistachio (Re)
5			x			x				x		x		x					x			x					x		x				5	#424 Red (Ra)	Pistachio (Re)
4		x				x				x				x				x			x		x			x			x				4	Scarlet (Re)	Pistachio (Re)
3		x				x				x				x				x			x		x			x			x				3	Scarlet (Re)	Pistachio (Re)
2		x						x		x				x		x							x		x							x	2	Poppy (H)	Pistachio (Re)
1		x	x	x	x	x	x		x	x	x	x	x	x	x		x	x	x	x	x	x		x	x	x	x	x	x	x	x	x	1	Poppy (H)	Pistachio (Re)
	32	31	30	29	28	27	26	25	24	23	22	21	20	19	18	17	16	15	14	13	12	11	10	9	8	7	6	5	4	3	2	1			

Chart 5

Chart 4.1 or Chart 4.2

R 1: k all 597 sts of the upper edge with Calypso (Re) for Version 1 or Marble Gemstone (Re) for Version 2 with 3.25 mm needles; adjust needle size to obtain gauge if necessary.

Inc 1 st by kfb from the 1st steek st and place SM (left tip; 2-st-marker).
Pick up and knit 309 sts on the left side.
At the bottom tip inc 2 sts and place SM (2-st-marker).
Pick up and knit 390 sts on the right side.

Inc 1 st by kfb from the 15th steek st and place SM (right tip; 2-st-marker).

R 2-6:

K the piping cord pattern with 3.25 mm needles; adjust needle size to obtain gauge if necessary.
The sts of the 2-st-markers are knit with 1 st each in the colours as mentioned. All these rounds do not feature any increases.

Forming the piping cord

Chart 4.1 or Chart 4.2:

R 7: k with Calypso (Re) for Version 1 or Marble Gemstone (Re) for Version 2 and knit each and every stitch together with the corresponding stitch of R 1 on the reverse side of the border. This round does not feature any increases.

BORDER PATTERN (SEE P. 150)

At each of the 2-st-markers inc 1 st on both sides by M1R and M1L.

The sts of the 2-st-markers are always knitted with BC.

Please be reminded to regularly increase (2-st-markers) at all three tips of the shawl.

Due to the continuous increases, the pattern must also be extended to the left and the right.

R 1-24: k the border pattern with BC and PC according to Chart 5.
R 25-30: k the piping cord pattern according to Chart 4.1 or 4.2 respectively. These rounds to not feature any increases.

Forming the outer piping cord

R 31: k each and every stitch together with the corresponding stitch of R 25 on the reverse side of the border with Calypso (Re) for Version 1 or Marble Gemstone (Re) for Version 2. This round does not feature any increases.

Reverse side of the border

Now all increases previously made at the three tips of the shawl border front (2-st markers) must be decreased.

In each R before and after the 2-st-marker 1 st each has to be decreased left-leaning (ssk) and right-leaning (k2tog) accordingly.

This way 6 sts are being decreased in each round.

Please follow the pattern repeats as created for the front side of the border.

R 32-55: k the border pattern with BC and PC according to Chart 5.
R 56: k with BC only. Cast-off all sts and sew them to the inside of the border.
See the description of the "knit-and-sew cast-off" method (cf. pages 24-26).

Finishing the shawl

Wash and block the shawl.

After drying the shawl, you might want to prepare tassels and sew them to the tips of the shawl.

DAHLIAS

The colours of a beautiful bouquet of tulips inspired me to make this shawl. Spring colours have a very special charisma and in combination with May green they are simply wonderful!

Yarn

Abbreviation	Yarn Manufacturer	Yardage/100g
G	Gardiner S08 Shetland (100% wool)	450 m/100g
G1	Gardiner SS11 Soft Shetland (100% wool)	565 m/100g
H	Harrisville New England Shetland (100% pure wool)	397 m/100g
J	Jamieson of Shetland Shetland Spindrift (100% pure Shetland wool)	420 m/100g
JU	Jamieson of Shetland Ultra (50% Shetland/50% lambswool)	776 m/100g
K	Knoll Supersoft (100% PURE NEW WOOL)	576 m/100g
SF	Lankava Esito worsted wool yarn (100% wool)	425 m/100g
Ra	Rauma Finull PT2 (100% Norwegian wool)	350 m/100g
Re	Rennie Supersoft (100% lambswool)	565 m/100g
ReU	Rennie Unique Shetland (100% lambswool)	450 m/100g
ReC	Rennie Supersoft Cashmere (87.5% lambswool/ 12.5% cashmere)	492 m/100g
LT	Tines 100% wool	350 m/100g

Shetland Spindrift, Supersoft (lambswool), pure new wool etc. The yardage of the different yarns varies. Further information can be found in the chapter concerning yarns and suppliers (see pp. 160-161).

Yarn kit "Dahlias" by Bärbel Salet VerstrickteKunst or

(Re), Clementine (K), Tangerine (J), Apricot (J), Sugarsnape (K), Blossom (J), Rose (J), #522 Flamingo (LT), Water Lily (H), Pink Lavender (G), #250 Lilac (LT), Heather Rose (Re)

420 g background colour(s) (BC)
7 x 60 g Leprechaun (J), New Lawn (Re), Kiwi (H), Garden Leaf (Re)*, #345 Jungle (LT), #458 Spring Green (Ra), Grass (G)

The amount of yarn required for the border and the pom-poms is included in the above.
Piping cord: * Garden Leaf (Re)

400 g pattern colour(s) (PC)
20 x 20 g Freesia (G), Aster (H), Cottage (Re), Red Clover (K), Geranium (K), Salmon (Re), Flame (J), Perfect Peach (Re), Jaffa

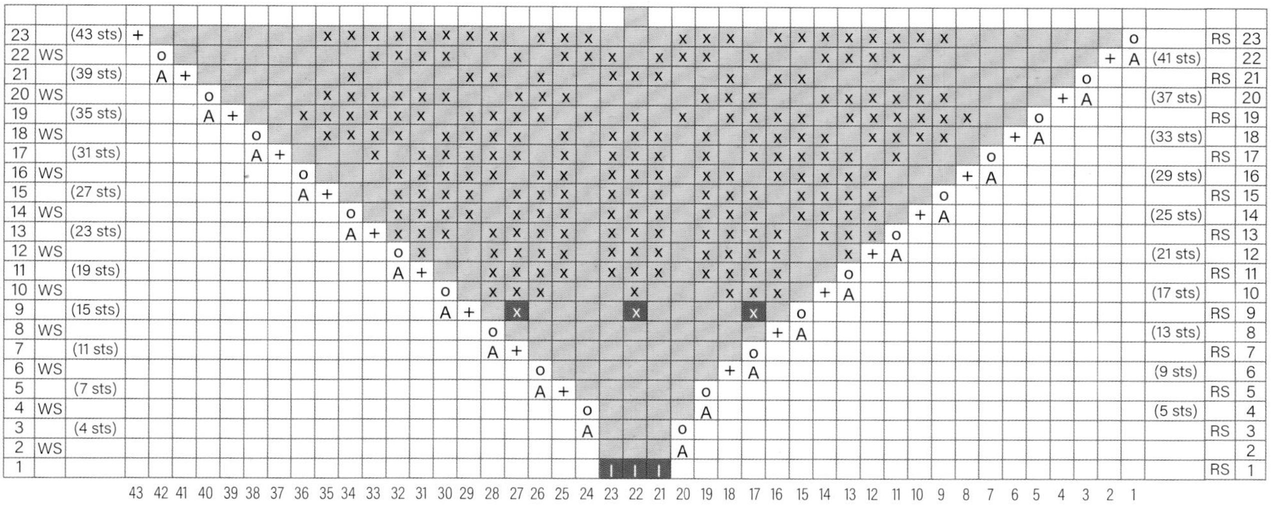

Chart 1

Row		Left	Right		Row
23		(43 sts) +	o … RS		23
22	WS	o	+ A (41 sts)		22
21		(39 sts) A +	o RS		21
20	WS	o	+ A (37 sts)		20
19		(35 sts) A +	o RS		19
18	WS	o	+ A (33 sts)		18
17		(31 sts) A +	o RS		17
16	WS	o	+ A (29 sts)		16
15		(27 sts) A +	o RS		15
14	WS	o	+ A (25 sts)		14
13		(23 sts) A +	o RS		13
12	WS	o	+ A (21 sts)		12
11		(19 sts) A +	o RS		11
10	WS	o	+ A (17 sts)		10
9		(15 sts) A +	o RS		9
8	WS	o	+ A (13 sts)		8
7		(11 sts) A +	o RS		7
6	WS	o	+ A (9 sts)		6
5		(7 sts) A +	o RS		5
4	WS	o	A (5 sts)		4
3		(4 sts) A	o RS		3
2	WS		A		2
1			RS		1

Column numbers (bottom, left to right): 43 42 41 40 39 38 37 36 35 34 33 32 31 30 29 28 27 26 25 24 23 22 21 20 19 18 17 16 15 14 13 12 11 10 9 8 7 6 5 4 3 2 1

Legend:

- **x** pattern colour(s)
- ▥ background colour(s)
- **I** cast-on stitches
- **x** pattern starting point
- **A** chain cast-on stitch
- **o** knit
- **+** purl bump increase
- RS right side row
- WS wrong side row

Arrangement of colours

The gradient colour schemes of both PC and BC are achieved with the help of previously prepared "magic balls", see the technical chapter, p. 13 ff. The wingspans are being determined individually.

Needles

3.25 mm circular needles (with different cable lengths); adjust needle size to obtain gauge if necessary.
DPNs might be useful at the beginning of the shawl.
3 sets of 3.25 mm circular needles with 100 cm cables for knitting the border; adjust needle size to obtain gauge if necessary.

Gauge

27 sts and 32 rows with 3.25 mm needles = 10 x 10 cm

Dimensions

Width 212 cm
Height 100 cm

Stitches

Stockinette stitch; two-colour Fair Isle knitting

Starting the shawl

R 1 cast-on row: co 3 sts with BC [I]
R 2 (WS): p 3 + chain cast-on 1 st [A]
R 3 (RS): k [o], k 3 sts = 4 sts, chain cast-on 1 st [A]
R 4 (WS): k [o], p 4 sts = 5 sts, chain cast-on 1 st [A]
R 5 (RS): From this row onwards 1 st is increased each at the beginning [A] and at the end [+].

K R 6 (WS) up to R 8 (WS).

K R 9 (RS): This row marks the beginning/starting point of the patterned section.

K R 10 (WS) up to and including R 23 (RS).

Integration of steek stitches

R 23 (RS/43 sts on needle): At the end of this row chain cast-on 15 steek sts, alternating between BC and PC. Close the row to a round. From now on all sts are k sts. Continue knitting either with DPNs or using the Magic Loop technique.

Please change to Chart 2 / R 24.

155

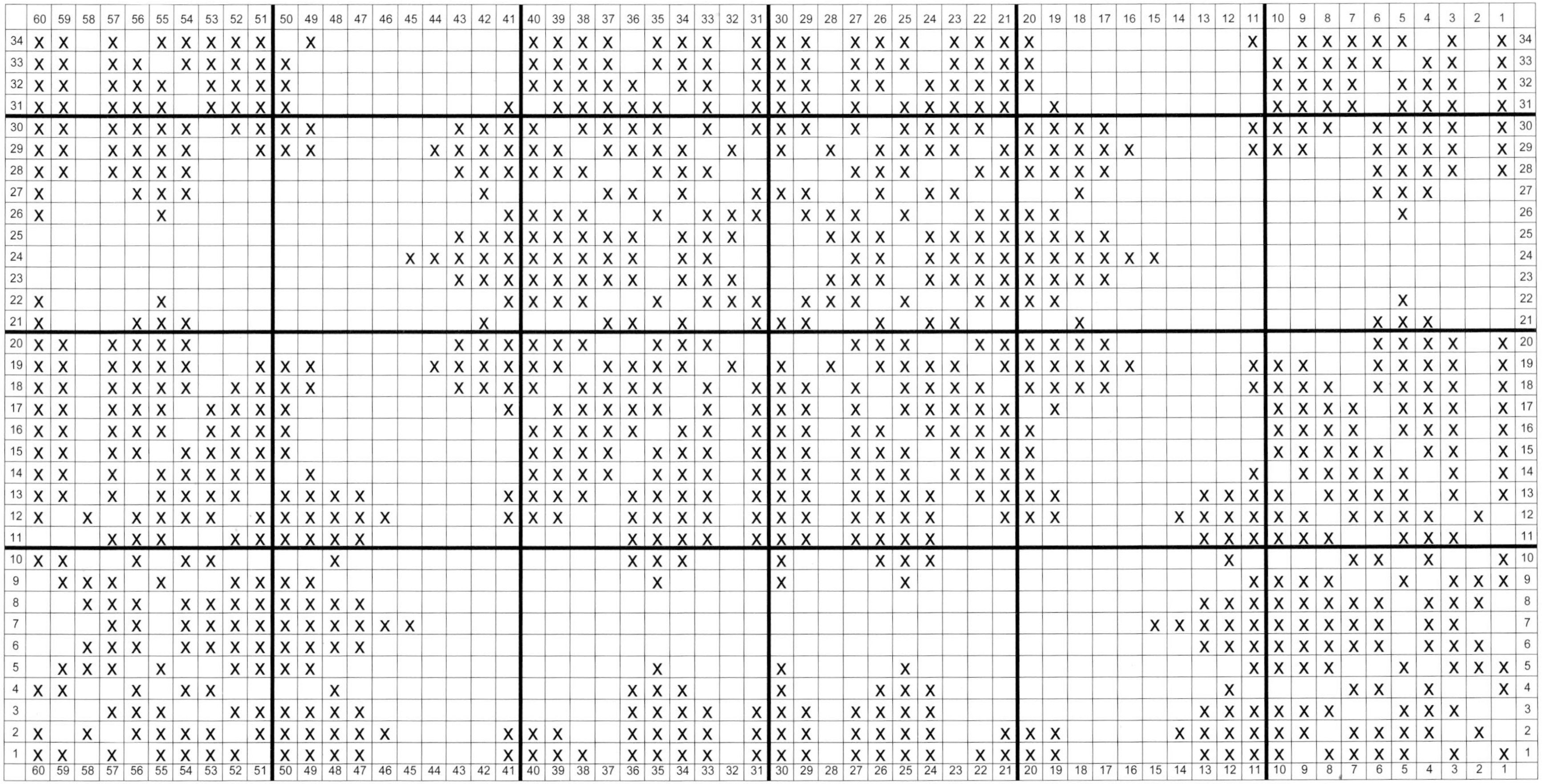

Chart 2

First round with steek stitches

Start knitting R 24 with the following partition (Chart 2):

» K from st 9 up to and including st 51.
» Place SM.
» K 14 steek sts according to the established colour scheme.
» Place SM.
» K the 15th steek st.

This first round with steek stitches does not feature any increase.

From R 25 onwards and all following rounds

» K all sts according to Chart 2/R 25.
» At the end of this R, inc 1 st by kfb from the last st.
» Move SM to the right needle.
» K 14 steek sts.
» Move SM to the right needle.
» Inc 1 st by kfb from the 15th steek stitch

As increases are regularly added, the pattern must also be extended to the right and left.

For better orientation, completed horizontal pattern repeats should be identified by the placement of SMs.

Once the first pattern repeat has been achieved hight-wise, start again with R 1.

In the end the shawl will be 279 rounds high (8 x 34 R of the complete pattern repeat plus one partial repeat from R 1 to and including R 7) and 552 sts wide.

The pattern is repeated 9 times horizontally in total (9 x 60 sts = 540 sts) plus the first 6 sts of a pattern repeat on the upper left tip and the last 6 sts of a pattern repeat on the upper right tip = 552 sts.

Cutting the steek

Bind off steek sts 2 until 14 inclusive. Moisten and block the steek. When dry, secure the steek and cut it open.

Border

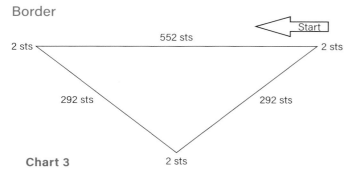

552 sts

2 sts   2 sts

292 sts   292 sts

Chart 3   2 sts

BC = green shades "magic ball"
PC = pastel shades "magic ball"

Piping cord

R 1: k all 552 sts of the upper edge with Garden Leaf (Re).

Inc 1 st by kfb from the 1st steek st and place SM (left tip; 2-st-marker).
Pick up and knit 292 sts on the left side.
At the bottom tip inc 2 sts and place SM (2-st-marker).
Pick up and knit 292 sts on the right side.

Inc 1 st by kfb from the 15th steek st and place SM (right tip; 2-st-marker).

R 2-5: k with Garden Leaf (Re).
The sts of the 2-st-markers are knit with 1 st each in the colours as mentioned. All these rounds do not feature any increases.

Forming the piping cord

R 6: k with Garden Leaf (Re) and knit each and every stitch together with the corresponding stitch of R 1 on the reverse side of the border. This round does not feature any increases.

	18	17	16	15	14	13	12	11	10	9	8	7	6	5	4	3	2	1	
46	X	X	X				X	X	X				X	X	X				46
45	X	X				X	X	X					X	X	X			X	45
44	X				X	X	X				X	X	X				X	X	44
43			X	X	X					X	X	X				X	X	X	43
42		X	X	X					X	X	X				X	X	X		42
41	X	X				X	X	X				X	X	X				X	41
40	X	X	X				X	X	X				X	X	X				40
39		X	X	X				X	X	X				X	X	X			39
38			X	X	X				X	X	X				X	X	X		38
37			X	X	X					X	X	X				X	X	X	37
36	X	X	X				X	X	X				X	X	X				36
35	X	X				X	X	X					X	X	X			X	35
34	X				X	X	X				X	X	X				X	X	34
33			X	X	X					X	X	X				X	X	X	33
32			X	X	X				X	X	X				X	X	X		32
31	X	X				X	X	X				X	X	X				X	31
30	X	X	X				X	X	X				X	X	X				30
29		X	X	X				X	X	X				X	X	X			29
28			X	X	X				X	X	X				X	X	X		28
27			X	X	X					X	X	X				X	X	X	27
26																			26
25																			25
24			**P**	**I**	**P**	**I**	**N**	**G**		**C**	**O**	**R**	**D**						24
23																			23
22																			22
21																			21
20	X	X	X				X	X	X				X	X	X				20
19	X	X				X	X	X				X	X	X				X	19
18	X				X	X	X				X	X	X				X	X	18
17			X	X	X					X	X	X				X	X	X	17
16			X	X	X				X	X	X				X	X	X		16
15	X	X				X	X	X				X	X	X				X	15
14	X	X	X				X	X	X				X	X	X				14
13		X	X	X				X	X	X				X	X	X			13
12			X	X	X				X	X	X				X	X	X		12
11			X	X	X					X	X	X				X	X	X	11
10	X	X	X				X	X	X				X	X	X				10
9	X	X				X	X	X				X	X	X				X	9
8	X				X	X	X				X	X	X				X	X	8
7			X	X	X					X	X	X				X	X	X	7
6			X	X	X				X	X	X				X	X	X		6
5	X	X				X	X	X				X	X	X				X	5
4	X	X	X				X	X	X				X	X	X				4
3		X	X	X				X	X	X				X	X	X			3
2			X	X	X				X	X	X				X	X	X		2
1				X	X	X				X	X	X				X	X	X	1
	18	17	16	15	14	13	12	11	10	9	8	7	6	5	4	3	2	1	

Chart 4

KNITTING THE BORDER PATTERN

At each of the 2-st-markers inc 1 st on both sides by M1R and M1L.

The sts of the 2-st-markers are always knitted with BC.

Please be reminded to regularly increase (2-st-markers) at all three tips of the shawl.

Due to the continuous increases, the pattern must also be extended to the left and the right.

R 1-20: k the border pattern with BC and PC according to Chart 4.
R 21-25: k the piping cord pattern with Garden Leaf (Re) only. These rounds to not feature any increases.

Forming the outer piping cord

R 26: k each and every stitch together with the corresponding stitch of R 21 on the reverse side of the border. This round does not feature any increases.

Reverse side of the border

Now all increases previously made at the three tips of the shawl border front (2-st markers) must be decreased.

In each R before and after the 2-st-marker 1 st each has to be decreased left-leaning (ssk) and right-leaning (k2tog) accordingly.

This way 6 sts are being decreased in each round.

Please follow the pattern repeats as created for the front side of the border.

R 27-46: k the border pattern with BC and PC.

Cast-off all sts and sew them to the inside of the border. See the description of the "knit-and-sew cast-off" method (see pp. 24-26).

Finishing the shawl

Wash and block the shawl.

After drying the shawl, you might want to prepare tassels and sew them to the tips of the shawl together with felted balls.

YARNS USED IN THIS BOOK AND MANUFACTURERS' WEBSITES

In my studio I have more than 360 different yarn colours from different manufacturers and spinning mills. The large number of shades makes it possible for me to create very smooth transitions for my colour gradient schemes.

Brierley Brothers Ltd (G + G1)

www.gardiner-yarns.co.uk
G = S08 Shetland (100% wool); yardage = 450 m/100g
G1 = SS11 Soft Shetland (100% wool); yardage = 492 m/100g

Harrisville Design (H)

www.harrisville.com
New England Shetland (100% pure wool); yardage = 397 m/100g

Jamieson's of Shetland (J + JU)

www.jamiesonsofshetland.co.uk
J = Shetland Spindrift (100% pure Shetland wool); yardage = 425 m/100g
JU = Ultra (50% Shetland/50% lambswool); yardage = 776 m/100g

Knoll (K)

www.knollyarns.com
Supersoft (100% PURE NEW WOOL); yardage= 576 m/100g

Lankava (SF)

www.lankava.fi
Esito worsted wool yarn (100% wool); yardage = 425 m/100g

Rauma (Ra)

www.raumagarn.no
Finull PT2 (100% Norwegian wool); yardage = 350 m/100g

J. C. Rennie (Re, ReU + ReC)

www.knitrennie.com
Re = Supersoft (100% lambswool); yardage = 492 m/100g
ReU = Unique Shetland (100% lambswool); yardage = 450 m/100g
ReC = Supersoft Cashmere (87.5% lambswool/ 12.5% cashmere); yardage = 492 m/100g

Tines (LT)

www.tines.lv/en/
100% wool; yardage = 350 m/100g

Abbreviation	Yarn Manufacturer	Yardage/100g
G	Gardiner S08 Shetland (100% wool)	450m/100g
G1	Gardiner SS11 Soft Shetland (100% wool)	565m/100g
H	Harrisville New England Shetland (100% pure wool)	397m/100g
J	Jamieson of Shetland Shetland Spindrift (100% pure Shetland wool)	420m/100g
JU	Jamieson of Shetland Ultra (50% Shetland/50% lambswool)	776m/100g
K	Knoll Supersoft (100% PURE NEW WOOL)	576m/100g
SF	Lankava Esito Worsted Wool Yarn (100% wool)	425m/100g
Ra	Rauma Finull PT2 (100% Norwegian wool)	350m/100g
Re	Rennie Supersoft (100% lambswool)	565m/100g
ReU	Rennie Unique Shetland (100% lambswool)	450m/100g
ReC	Rennie Supersoft Cashmere (87.5% lambswool/12.5% cashmere)	492m/100g
LT	Tines 100% wool	350m/100g

The yarns for all shawls contained in this book have been provided exclusively by VerstrickteKunst – Bärbel Salet.